D0177841

Notes from the Jam Cupboard

Notes from the Jam Cupboard

Mary Tregellas

NEW
HOLLAND

First published in 2012 by New Holland Publishers (UK) Ltd
London • Cape Town • Sydney • Auckland

Garfield House, 86–88 Edgware Rd, London W2 2EA, United Kingdom

80 McKenzie Street, Cape Town 8001, South Africa

Unit 1, 66 Gibbes Street, Chatswood, NSW 2067, Australia

218 Lake Road, Northcote, Auckland, New Zealand

Text copyright © 2012 Mary Tregellas
Copyright © 2012 New Holland Publishers (UK) Ltd

Mary Tregellas has asserted her moral right to be identified as the author of this work.

Notes from the Jam Cupboard was created for New Holland Publishers (UK) Ltd
by Geoff Borin and Samantha Stanley (www.made-to-measure-books.co.uk)

The publishers would like to thank HarperCollins Ltd for the use of the quote from
Paddington at Large by Michael Bond on page 74.
Reprinted by permission of HarperCollins Publishers Ltd
© 1962 Michael Bond

ISBN 978 1 78009 006 1

Publisher: Clare Sayer
Editor: Marilyn Inglis
Production: Laurence Poos
Photography: John Davis (except pages 6, 7, 25, 26, 28, 35, 46, 48, 53, 61, 69, 96, 109,
150, 180, 181, 183, 188, 189, 192 – Mary Tregellas/1, 23, 75 – Geoff Borin)

10 9 8 7 6 5 4 3 2 1

Reproduction by Pica Digital PTE Ltd, Singapore

Printed and bound in Singapore by Craft Print International Ltd

Contents

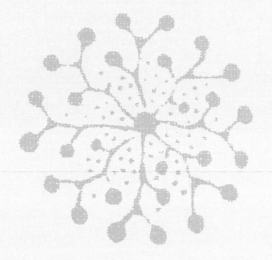

Introduction

'This has gone beyond a hobby now, this is an obsession,' announced my brother, finding me at the jam pan at 7am one Saturday morning. How did it come to this, that my first thoughts when waking early on a weekend revolve around what to bottle before breakfast? I suppose it started in childhood. My mother was a refugee from Czechoslovakia and would entertain us with stories of hours spent in her grandmother's garden where the trees hung heavy with apricots and redcurrants grew in abundance. She was also especially fond of jam – not the jellied mass of sugar and pectin so prevalent in 1970s Britain, but the kind of preserve where the fruit is the star. Occasionally our village shop would sell cut-price conserves from Poland or Bulgaria – her eyes would light up and she would buy as much as we could carry home. For a special occasion we would visit the delicatessen in the nearby town, an Aladdin's cave of delights including jars of delicious morello cherry jam. But these were rare treats, for money was in short supply. Nothing went to waste, and if we could grow things in our small garden or gather something for free, so much the better. Dandelion leaves enlivened salads, young nettles were picked for soup and bunches of herbs dried to use throughout the year. Then came visits to relatives in Germany, whose cellar was lined with shelves of preserves and bottled fruits. Nothing I've made has ever come close to my Aunt Hanne's great Parfait jars of apricot and strawberry jam. And, of course, my mother would make her own – redcurrant jelly in memory of her grandmother's garden, pear and ginger jam, tomato chutney…

Left to right

The four sisters (left to right) Tante Jenny, Tante Trude, Tante Betty, my grandmother Antonie.

Renate Lindenthal (aged 4) with her grandfather, Jarcová, Moravia (Czechoslovakia), 1930.

Renate Lindenthal, Beskydy Mountains, Moravia, 1930.

My own jam-making started with an over-enthusiastic greengage tree and the pleasure of giving my jam-loving mother a never-ending supply. Then we acquired an allotment and, with it, further challenges: what to do with a glut of courgettes? (Chutney!) Or tomatoes? (Ketchup!) Add to that my childhood passion for picking wild fruit and the guardianship of my family home in Devon (whose small garden still yields the most delicious pears in the world), and the result is a cupboard full of jams, jellies, chutneys, sauces and other delights to spread on toast, liven up a cheese sandwich or accompany pies and sausages.

I have come to realize a simple fact: preserve-making makes me happy. Chopping up a pile of fruit or vegetables, cooking them up with sugar, spices and vinegar and thereby transforming them into something both delicious and attractive is intensely pleasing. I view all cookery as a form of alchemy, but perhaps none more so than the art of preserving, when the flavours and aromas of something short-lived are captured in a pot to be savoured throughout the coming year. But the preserves themselves are only part of the story. There is matchmaking to be done too – whether it's bringing together the happiest of old couples such as toast and marmalade or cheese and pickle, or forming new introductions. They also come into their own as ingredients in baked puddings, cakes and savoury dishes. I hope that this book will reacquaint you with some old favourites, encourage you to try new things, and inspire you to come up with a few ideas of your own.

Left to right

My mother, Tante Betty and my father, Innsbruck, Austria, 1962.

My brother John, father Frank, mother Renate and me, 1969.

The Tasting Panel – my family – Ben with (left to right) James, Alexander and Edward.

Preserving the seasons

Last year our fridge-freezer packed up. While the insurance claim was underway, we lived for several weeks with a small borrowed refrigerator that just about coped with everyday essentials. Such an apparently small change to our kitchen had a huge impact on our shopping and eating habits. We reverted to buying small quantities daily, and nothing was bought without considering how to store and cook it. I rather enjoyed the challenge.

My favourite childhood book was Laura Ingalls Wilder's *Little House in the Big Woods*; I loved her stories of stocking up for times ahead. She describes a whole range of preserving techniques, skills that are part of a centuries-old way of life: smoking, freezing, cheesemaking, collecting sap to make into maple syrup, storing those fruit and vegetables that keep and preserving the rest in jams and pickles. Skip forward 140 years and how things have changed! With most produce available year round, and ever larger fridges and freezers in which to store it, the seasons have become blurred. But concerns over food miles and carbon footprints, and a growing appreciation of good food, simply cooked, are helping to put the emphasis back on fresh, local, seasonal produce. And we are rediscovering some of the old ways. We may no longer *need* to bake our own bread, to pick wild berries, to make jam, but we can have a lot of fun doing it.

Let the seasons be your guide: January and February are marmalade months, with wonderful, bitter Seville oranges in season; spring and early summer see the appearance of rhubarb and gooseberries, while creamy elderflowers cry out to be made into cordial. Then come the first strawberries, heralding the summer's mad whirl of berries, stone fruit and vegetables. In early autumn, apples and pears take centre stage, and there are still plenty of hedgerow goodies to be foraged. By late autumn things are slowing down; the shelves groaning with jars and bottles of beautiful homemade preserves to enjoy throughout the year ahead. Grab your wooden spoon: preserving is back in town!

Useful equipment

Many preserves can be made with a bare minimum of equipment – a pan, a wooden spoon and some jars – but there are some other handy tools to have.

Preserving pan

If you are going to invest in just one thing, then let it be a stainless steel preserving pan (or maslin pan). These are large deep pans with sloped sides, which allow liquid to reduce more quickly and lessen the danger of hot preserves splashing everywhere. A large, heavy-based stainless steel saucepan is the best alternative. Avoid aluminium pans, which can affect the taste.

Wooden spoon

One with a long handle is best – hot preserves can spit, so it is a good idea to keep a little distance between them and your hands. Avoid metal spoons, which can react with ingredients and discolour the preserve.

Jam thermometer

These clip to the side of the pan and are used to prevent over-boiling and check the temperature of preserves to ensure that they have reached the correct temperature for setting. I rarely use mine for this, but do find it useful when pasteurizing cordials.

Jam funnel

This is a special wide-mouthed funnel that makes it much easier to fill jars without spills. A narrow funnel is useful for filling bottles too. An alternative is to pour the preserve into jars using a heatproof jug.

Jelly bag and stand

A fine-woven bag is used to strain the juice from the pulp when making jelly and cordial. Often sold with a stand, or with loops for hanging, they can also be attached to an upturned stool with a bowl underneath to catch the juice. Alternatively, line a large strainer with a double layer of muslin or fine cotton (such as an old, clean tea towel) and suspend over a deep bowl. The jelly bag should always be scalded in a saucepan of boiling water just before use.

Muslin or spice ball

Use a piece of muslin for tying whole spices together. A spice ball is a metal mesh container, usually on a chain, which clips to the side of the pan (shown opposite).

Slotted spoon

Scum can form when jams and jellies are cooking so a slotted spoon is useful for skimming it off the surface. It is also helpful in fishing out stones from cherries, damsons and other stone fruit.

Kitchen scissors

I find kitchen scissors invaluable in preserve-making, from slicing cooked peel for marmalade and cutting rhubarb into chunks, to chopping chillies and dried apricots.

Mouli

Making purée with a stainless steel mouli is a lot easier on the arms than pressing ingredients through a sieve.

Jars, bottles, lids and covers

It is fine to re-use jam jars and bottles, as long as they have no chips or cracks, so save them up or ask your friends and neighbours to give you theirs. The most useful sizes are the 340 g (12 oz) and 227 g (8 oz) jars. Avoid any that contained very pungent things in a former life.

Lids can also be re-used, though with second-hand lids it is advisable to cover the jar with a cellophane circle or cling film first. Select lids that are not tainted by the smell of the previous preserve – a whiff of gherkins is not great on strawberry jam. For chutneys and pickles, use lids with vinegar-proof linings as vinegar will corrode metal. You can buy new lids separately, and waxed circles, cellophane covers and elastic bands in packs. Place waxed circles (waxed side down) on hot preserves immediately after potting to form a seal.

A note on ingredients

Fruit and vegetables

There is a common misconception that second-rate fruit is suitable for jam – not so. For jam- and jelly-making, fruit should be just ripe or slightly under ripe, so that the flavour is at its best and the pectin content has not started to wane. Riper fruit and vegetables are suitable for chutneys, ketchups and cordials.

Rinse and prepare produce just before using; drain and dry well. Discard any squashy berries, and cut away bruises from hard fruits. Frozen produce is great for preserves: cook from frozen and adjust the cooking time accordingly.

Try to obtain at least some of your fruit and vegetables locally. Gardens, pick-your-own farms and farmers' markets are good places to start. Barter with your friends and neighbours – you are sure to find someone with produce to spare.

Sugars

It is the magical combination of sugar, acid and pectin that makes a good set. A high proportion of sugar also acts as a preservative, so don't be tempted to reduce the amount.

High-pectin fruits include cooking apples, redcurrants, blackcurrants, quinces, cranberries, gooseberries, damsons; medium-pectin fruits include raspberries,
apricots, greengages, plums, early blackberries; and low-pectin fruits are cherries, strawberries, pears, late blackberries, peaches and rhubarb.

For jams, jellies, marmalades and cordials, white granulated sugar serves most purposes, although brown sugar is delicious in marmalades.

Jam sugar contains added pectin and can be useful with fruits that are not good setters, such as strawberries and cherries. Preserving sugar has larger crystals and supposedly makes the clearest preserves, though I never use it.

For chutneys and sauces, various types of brown sugar (demerara, light and dark muscovado) are more commonly used, giving a deeper colour and flavour, though white granulated sugar works too.

Spices

Key ingredients in chutneys and sauces, spices give warmth, heat and fragrance to any recipe. Ready ground spices are convenient but a little less aromatic. When using whole spices, you have two choices: either tie them in muslin or place in a spice ball and let them swim around in the preserve, infusing it with their flavour; or, for the most flavoursome and potent results, toast the spices in a dry frying pan for 2–3 minutes, then grind in a spice mill or pestle and mortar and add to the preserve.

Vinegars

Vinegar's acidity gives it the power to preserve, since micro-organisms cannot grow in an acidic environment. Most types of vinegar are suitable for savoury preserves. Red and white wine vinegars are good all-rounders and work well in most recipes. Strong-tasting malt vinegars have long been used in preserving. Clear distilled malt vinegar is a good choice if you want to keep the colour of the original ingredients. Cider vinegar has a fruity taste, and is slightly less acidic than wine and malt varieties. Balsamic vinegar has a lower acidity, so is not suitable as a preservative, though it can be added for flavour.

Cold remedy

As well as its uses in chutney-making, cider vinegar is a magical ingredient for curing all kinds of ills. My mother's favourite cure for colds and flu was to drink hot cider vinegar and honey. Put two teaspoons of cider vinegar in a mug with a level tablespoon of honey. Top up with boiling water and stir until the honey is dissolved. Sip the hot drink slowly, inhaling the steam as you do so.

General preserving tips

I have a very small kitchen. No fancy equipment. No team of test chefs, just me and the Tasting Panel. And I haven't had a single cookery lesson in my life – so I can confidently say that preserve-making is something for everyone to try. Some can be made in an hour, start to finish; others take time and a little advance planning.

Jams

The usual method for jam-making is to cook fruit slowly until it is soft and the juices are flowing. It should be stirred frequently at the start, to prevent catching. The pan is then removed from the heat, sugar is added and stirred until thoroughly dissolved. The jam is boiled rapidly (known as a 'full rolling boil') until setting point is reached. Setting points vary from fruit to fruit, and other factors can affect it too – the size and type of pan, the ripeness of the fruit – so, although the individual recipes indicate an approximate time, it is necessary to test for a set with each batch to be sure (page 18).
• Do not fill the pan much more than half full, as the mixture can bubble up quite spectacularly.
• Do not stir jam (or jelly) too often during the boiling stage, as this lowers the temperature (a high temperature is needed to reach setting point).

• Adding fresh lemon juice to low-pectin fruits can help to achieve a set, and it brightens the flavour.
• A knob of butter, added to jams just after stirring in the sugar, can prevent scum forming. If you choose not to add the butter, you will need to skim off the scum. Wait until the end and skim in one go to avoid wastage.

Marmalades

The key to a good citrus marmalade is to cook the peel thoroughly before adding sugar, or the final preserve will be tough. There are two ways to make marmalade: either cook the fruit whole or shred the peel before cooking. To tell if the cooked peel is soft enough: with whole fruit, there should be no resistance when piercing with a fork; with shreds, you should be able to crush them easily between thumb and finger. Once the peel is softened, the method is much the same as jam – dissolve sugar and boil rapidly until a setting point is reached. See page 76 for more information on marmalade-making.

Curds

Fruit curds are soft and creamy preserves made from the juice and zest of citrus fruits, or the purée of other fruit varieties. The juice or

purée is whisked together with butter, sugar and eggs in a double boiler or in a heatproof bowl set over a pan of simmering water until the mixture coats the back of a spoon. Curds need careful attention while cooking to ensure they do not curdle. Make in small batches because they keep for only about four weeks in the fridge.

Cordials

Fruit that is too ripe for jam- or jelly-making is fine for cordials, since there is no setting point to worry about. The process starts in the same way as for jelly – cook the fruit with a little water until juicy, then strain through a jelly bag. Dissolve sugar in the strained juice and bottle. Cordials will keep for one to two months only in the fridge, but you can extend their keeping times by freezing and pasteurizing.

Freezing: allow the cordial to cool, then fill clean plastic bottles, leaving a gap at the top to allow for expansion as the cordial freezes. They should keep up to a year.

Pasteurizing: you will need a very deep saucepan, a sugar thermometer and bottles that are not too tall. After filling the bottles, screw the lids on lightly. Put a folded tea towel in the bottom of the pan and stand the bottles on it. They should not touch each other. Fill the pan with warm water to within 2.5 cm (1 in) of the tops, and heat the water to sterilizing point, 88°C (190°F). Maintain this temperature for 20 minutes, then remove the bottles and tighten the lids. Cordials processed this way should keep for up to a year, stored somewhere cool and dark. Refrigerate after opening.

Chutneys

Fruits and vegetables are cooked slowly with vinegar, sugar and spices until soft and well reduced. Depending on the ingredients, this can take up to two hours, so do not abandon the pan, especially in the later stages when it is more prone to catch and burn. Chutney is ready when a spoon drawn through it leaves a trail. It will thicken a bit more when cooled. If you can wait, leave chutneys to mature for a few weeks before eating – they will mellow and taste less vinegary. Most chutneys will keep for at least a year, and beyond, though they may discolour a little.

Jellies

One of the joys of jelly-making is that it requires minimal preparation; just wash and chop the fruit roughly (no peeling or de-seeding required). The fruit is cooked with water to release the juice and then strained through a jelly bag for several hours or overnight. The juice is then measured and cooked with sugar until it reaches setting point. The usual sugar-to-juice ratio is between 450–600 g (1–1 lb 5 oz) of sugar to 600 ml (1 pint) juice.

Acid and pectin are essential in the setting of jams and jellies. I like soft jams, so rarely worry about achieving a firm set, but nobody wants runny jelly and jellies need pectin in order to set well. Use high-pectin fruits (or combine with those that are), or add pectin in liquid or powdered form. Adding tart cooking apples or freshly squeezed lemon juice can help.

Squeezing the bag yields more juice but turns the jelly cloudy, so for a crystal-clear preserve, leave the jelly bag to drip. This is especially desirable when making light-coloured jellies, such as apple and quince. However, with darker varieties, such as bramble, I squeeze or press down the contents of the jelly bag with a spoon. As the jelly is very dark, a little cloudiness goes unnoticed.

Ketchups and sauces

A little like chutneys, these are made from fruit, vegetables, vinegar, sugar and spices, but turned into a smooth purée by rubbing through a sieve or a mouli, and then cooked until they reach the desired consistency.

Sterilizing

Jars and bottles should be sterilized just before filling to prevent the growth of bacteria. Do not use any that have cracks or chips. The method I always use is as follows: wash well in hot soapy water, rinse thoroughly and drain. Place on a baking tray in a cold oven, turn it to 150°C (300°F) and leave them for 15–20 minutes – try to time it so that the jars are ready at roughly the same time as the preserve. Most metal jam-jar lids, including many lined ones, can be sterilized in the same way, or placed in boiling water for two minutes and then thoroughly dried with kitchen paper. Jars and bottles can also be sterilized in a dishwasher, using the hottest cycle.

Alternatively, place the jars in a saucepan and cover with warm water. Bring to the boil and boil for 10 minutes, then drain and leave to air dry.

Testing for a set

(For jams, jellies and marmalades.) Always take the pan off the heat while you are testing for a set.

The wrinkle test: place a saucer in the freezer for a few minutes. Put half a teaspoon of preserve on the chilled plate and return to the freezer for a minute. Then push the preserve gently with your finger – it will wrinkle if setting point has been reached. If not, boil for another 2–3 minutes and test again. I find this method to be the most reliable.

The thermometer test: the setting point of jam and marmalade is 105°C (220°F). If your preserve has reached this temperature, in theory setting point has been reached. (In my experience this is not always the case!)

The flake test: dip a wooden spoon in the preserve, let it cool for a few seconds, then let it drop off the spoon. If the preserve forms flakes that hang on the edge of the spoon, setting point has been reached.

Potting

Remove any scum from the preserve with a metal spoon. Make sure you have everything ready – funnel, ladle, jars. (I keep the jars on the baking tray when filling to catch any spills.) Ladle the hot preserve into the hot jars, filling them almost to the top. With thicker preserves such as chutneys, you may need to remove air pockets by pushing down with a teaspoon. Place a waxed disc (wax side down) on top of the preserve, cover with a cellophane circle if using, then screw the lid on tightly. Use an oven glove or tea towel, as the jars will be hot. Leave to cool and label.

Preserves that contain large pieces of fruit should be left to cool for 15 minutes before potting, so that the fruit/shreds do not all rise to the top of the jar.

Storing

Most jams, jellies, chutneys and marmalades will keep for at least a year. They should be stored somewhere cool, dark and dry. Once opened, all preserves should be kept in the fridge and eaten within a few weeks. See individual recipes for specific storage instructions.

Luscious

Strawberries, raspberries, gooseberries, currants and cranberries

Jam

'And the Quangle Wangle said
To himself on the Crumpetty Tree,
Jam; and Jelly; and bread;
Are the best of food for me!'

Edward Lear (1812–1888) 'The Quangle Wangle's Hat'

I remember my mother scrutinizing jam-jar labels before making a purchase. She was picky – only those listing fruit and sugar as their sole ingredients made it into her shopping basket, and these were surprisingly hard to find. Yet the recipe for jam really is that basic: roughly equal quantities of fruit and sugar, perhaps a little lemon or redcurrant juice to help with setting and cut through the sweetness, and careful cooking. It can be eaten immediately, but usually keeps for at least a year. You don't need to be a master chef to attempt it, and no special equipment is required – just a large pan and a wooden spoon. Once you have mastered the art, you will want to turn everything into jam. And having tasted your homemade jam, you will want to put it in and on everything – bread, waffles, cakes, tarts…

If you have never made a pot of jam in your life before, the fruits of the forest jam (page 25) is an excellent recipe to start with. It requires virtually no preparation and not much cooking time either, yet it produces a jam that is a firm favourite with the Tasting Panel and also features in the delicious summer fruit trifle (but more of that later…).

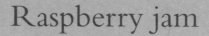

Raspberry jam

Here's a recipe to dispel the myth that jam-making is complicated and time-consuming, and it's a beautiful preserve too. Enjoy the colours while you're cooking – bright and vibrant at the start, it deepens into a rich pinky-red, and the perfume is divine. This also works very well made with frozen raspberries.

1 kg (2 lb 4 oz) raspberries
juice of 2 lemons
1 kg (2 lb 4 oz) granulated sugar
a knob of butter

Makes 6–7 x 227 g (8 oz) jars
Keeps for 12 months

1 Put the raspberries and lemon juice in the pan and cook over a very gentle heat for a few minutes (up to 10 minutes if you are using frozen berries), stirring frequently to prevent it catching on the sides of the pan.

2 Remove from the heat and add the sugar, stirring until dissolved, then add the butter. Return the pan to the heat and bring to the boil. Cook at a full rolling boil for 5 minutes, then test for a set and pot into hot sterilized jars (page 18).

TIP

As this is a speedy recipe, make sure your jars are sterilized in time. I wash mine and put them in the oven when I start cooking.

Edward's comment: 'Looks like the kind of jam that pops out in Wallace and Gromit. Mmm… Fantastic!'

Fruits of the forest jam

This beautiful preserve is one of the quickest, easiest jam recipes ever. It's a particular favourite with children, perhaps because there's an element of lucky dip about it – you might get a strawberry in one spoonful, a cherry in another. Delicious on fresh bread or scones, it also makes a wonderful filling for a cake.

1.5 kg (3 lb 5 oz) mixed berries
(fresh or frozen)

juice of 2 lemons

100 ml (3½ fl oz) water

1.5 kg (3 lb 5 oz) granulated sugar

a knob of butter

Makes 7 x 340 g (12 oz) jars

Keeps for 12 months

1 Use any combination of berries as long as you have the required weight. Put the fruit and lemon juice in the preserving pan, add the water and cook over a moderate heat for 10–12 minutes (a little longer for frozen fruit). Stir occasionally until very soft.

2 Remove from the heat and stir in the sugar until it has dissolved, then add the butter.

3 Bring to the boil and cook at a rolling boil for about 5 minutes, then test for a set (page 18). If setting point hasn't been reached, boil again for 2–3 minutes and test again. Leave to stand for 5 minutes, then pot up (page 18).

Strawberry jam

The quest for a really good strawberry jam was a driving force in my early jam-making days, since the kind of preserve I want (soft set, with big pieces of fruit and a delicious aroma) is not easy to find. Every summer my challenge is to make enough of this delicious preserve to last the year. I've tried various recipes; here are my two favourites.

Recipe 1

1.6 kg (3 lb 8 oz) strawberries, hulled (halve or quarter any large ones)

juice of 2 lemons

1.3 kg (3 lb) granulated sugar

a knob of butter

Makes approximately 7 x 340 g (12 oz) jars

Keeps for 12 months

1 Put the strawberries and lemon juice in a preserving pan and cook over a gentle heat for about 10–15 minutes, stirring occasionally.

2 Remove from the heat and add the sugar, stirring until dissolved, then add the butter and stir in.

3 Return the pan to the heat and bring to the boil. Cook at a full rolling boil for about 20 minutes, then test for a set (page 18). Leave to stand for 15 minutes, then stir to distribute the fruit before potting up (page 18).

TIP

Unless the strawberries are very dirty, wipe rather than wash them. Strawberries become easily waterlogged and you do not need extra liquid.

Recipe 2

1.5 kg (3 lb 5 oz) strawberries, hulled (halve or quarter any large ones)

juice of 3 lemons or 300 ml (10 fl oz) unsweetened redcurrant juice

1.5 kg (3 lb 5 oz) granulated sugar

a knob of butter

Makes approximately 7 x 340 g (12 oz) jars

Keeps for 12 months

1 Put the strawberries, juice and sugar in a large bowl and stir together well. Mash slightly with a fork or potato masher, but leave plenty of large pieces. Cover with a clean cloth and leave for at least 15 minutes (a couple of hours is fine).

2 Tip the mixture into a preserving pan and bring to the boil, stirring frequently. Cook over a medium–high heat for 15–20 minutes, stirring occasionally. Stir in the butter.

3 Test for a set (page 18). It may need a few minutes more, especially if the strawberries are large and very juicy. Leave to stand for 15 minutes before potting up (page 18).

VARIATIONS

Strawberry jam with passion fruit

The slight tartness of the passion fruit complements the sweetness of the strawberries, and the seeds add a pleasing crunch.

You need one passion fruit for each 500 g (1 lb 2 oz) strawberries. Scoop the pulp and juice into a bowl with a teaspoon. Once the jam has reached setting point and is off the heat, stir in the passion fruit.

Strawberry jam with wild strawberries

Replace a few of the larger berries with some intensely flavoured wild or alpine strawberries – you won't need many to impart a heavenly flavour and aroma.

Gooseberry and elderflower jam

Elderflowers are still in season when early gooseberries appear, which may account for their traditional pairing. I usually make this with tart green berries; if you use a sweeter variety, you may need to reduce the sugar content. Gooseberries are pectin-rich and set well. If no flowers are to be had, use elderflower cordial.

2 kg (4 lb 8 oz) gooseberries (topped and tailed)

1.3 litres (2 pints) water

8–10 elderflower heads or 4 tbsps elderflower cordial

2.7 kg (6 lb) sugar, or 2.25 kg (5 lb) if using sweet berries

Makes about 10 x 340 g (12 oz) jars

Keeps for 12 months

1 Put the gooseberries and water in a preserving pan with the elderflower heads and cook over a moderate heat for 20 minutes or so until the gooseberries are really soft.

2 Take the pan off the heat, remove the flowerheads with a slotted spoon and discard. Add the sugar and stir until dissolved.

3 Return to the heat and bring to the boil. Cook at a full rolling boil for 10 minutes, then test for a set (page 18). If you are using cordial rather than flowers, stir it in at this stage. Pot into hot sterilized jars (page 18).

TIPS

I use a small pair of scissors to top and tail gooseberries. With frozen gooseberries, a thumbnail is probably all you need to do the job.

For a speedy gooseberry fool for four people, whip 300 ml (10 fl oz) double cream until thick, but not too stiff, and fold in a few spoons of this jam.

Blueberry jam *with a dash of lime*

Our summer holidays are often spent in central Europe where there is plenty of wild treasure to be found, especially blueberries. If we don't find many, I stew them with a little sugar and serve them hot over vanilla ice cream. A good haul, on the other hand, means jam! This recipe also works perfectly with shop-bought blueberries (fresh or frozen).

1.3 kg (3 lb) blueberries

4 limes, juice and zest

juice of ½ lemon

175 ml (6 fl oz) water

1.3 kg (3 lb) granulated sugar

150 ml (5 fl oz) liquid pectin

Makes 7–8 x 340 g (12 oz) jars

Keeps for 12 months

1 Put the blueberries, lime juice, lemon juice and water in a preserving pan and cook over a moderate heat for about 10 minutes until the blueberries are really soft.

2 Take the pan off the heat, add the sugar and stir until it is dissolved. Return the pan to the heat and bring to the boil. Cook at a full rolling boil for 4 minutes then add the pectin and boil for another minute or two.

3 Test for a set and pot into hot sterilized jars (page 18).

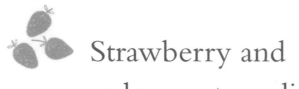

Strawberry and redcurrant cordial

Making cordial is a similar process to jelly-making, but as it doesn't need to set you can use very ripe fruit. The combination of sweet strawberries and tart redcurrants is, to my mind, pretty perfect and the colour is gorgeous. Dilute with water; add to vodka or champagne, or drizzle over creamy puddings.

850 g (1 lb 14 oz) strawberries

850 g (1 lb 14 oz) redcurrants

juice of ½ lemon

450 ml (16 fl oz) water

600–700 g (1 lb 5 oz–1 lb 9 oz) granulated sugar

Makes about 1.2 litres (2 pints)

Keeps for 2 months, unopened, in the fridge

1 Put the fruit, lemon juice and water in a large pan. Heat almost to boiling point, stirring, then lower to a gentle simmer for about 20 minutes until the fruit is very soft. Squash the fruit with the back of a spoon while it is simmering to release all the juice.

2 Pour into a scalded jelly bag (page 12) and leave it to drip for a few hours or overnight. Squeeze the bag to extract any remaining juice.

3 Measure the juice and pour it into a clean pan. You should have around 1 litre (1¾ pints). Add 600 g (1 lb 5 oz) of the sugar and taste. Add more if necessary. Heat gently and stir until the sugar is completely dissolved. Scrape down the sides of the pan with a spatula now and then. Bottle immediately in hot sterilized bottles (page 18) to within 1 cm (½ in) of the top. Leave to cool and then refrigerate.

TIP

To extend its shelf life, pasteurize the cordial or freeze it in clean plastic bottles (page 16–17).

Gooseberry chutney

My mother's friend Helga gave me a bag of plump, translucent gooseberries in shades from greeny-pink to dark red – almost too beautiful to eat. After enjoying their beauty for a couple of days, I made this chutney. It goes very well with fish, especially mackerel, and is delicious with a mild goats' cheese.

1 piece cinnamon bark

1 tsp mustard seeds

¾ tsp black peppercorns

6 allspice berries

300 ml (10 fl oz) white wine vinegar or cider vinegar

750 g (1 lb 10 oz) white granulated sugar

3 cm (1¼ in) fresh root ginger, peeled and grated

juice and grated zest of 1 lime

500 g (1 lb 2 oz) onions, peeled and chopped

1 kg (2 lb 4 oz) gooseberries, topped and tailed

Makes about 7 x 227 g (8 oz) jars

Keeps for 12 months

1 Lightly crush the spices in a pestle and mortar and tie together in a piece of muslin or put in a spice basket (page 12).

2 Put the vinegar, sugar, ginger and spice bag in a large pan and heat gently until the sugar has dissolved. Add the lime juice and zest and leave to infuse for 20 minutes.

3 Add the onions and gooseberries, bring to the boil and then reduce to a simmer. Cook for 50–60 minutes, stirring frequently until the mixture is well reduced and thickened (though it will still be fairly runny). Leave to cool for about 10 minutes then pot into hot sterilized jars (page 18).

TIP

You'll have time to chop the onions while the vinegar mixture is infusing.

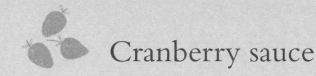

Cranberry sauce

Cranberry sauce gets an annual outing at Christmas and is otherwise largely forgotten, but it's a great preserve to have in your store cupboard all year round. It's delicious with game dishes or Schnitzel (page 40), and fantastic with a baked Camembert or in a Brie, bacon and spinach sandwich. It is also a traditional accompaniment to Kaiserschmarren (page 55).

1 kg (2 lb 4 oz) cranberries

zest and juice of 2 oranges

100 ml (3½ fl oz) water

1 kg (2 lb 4 oz) granulated sugar

a pinch of ground cinnamon

a pinch of mixed spice

Makes 5–6 x 340 g (12 oz) jars

Keeps for 12 months

1 Pick over the cranberries and discard any that are really squashy. Put them in a pan with the orange juice and water.

2 Cover and cook gently for 10–15 minutes, stirring from time to time. The cranberries will pop pleasingly.

3 Remove the pan from the heat and stir in the sugar, orange zest and spices, then return to the heat and boil rapidly for 3–5 minutes. The sauce will spit furiously when stirred at this stage so exercise caution. Test for a set, then pot into hot sterilized jars (page 18).

The evolution of the trifle

'That most wonderful object of domestic art called trifle…
with its charming confusion of cream and cake and almonds
and jam and jelly and wine and cinnamon and froth.'

Oliver Wendell Holmes, 1861

The first known trifle recipe dates from the late 1500s, and early versions were little more than thick cream sweetened with sugar, flavoured with spices, rosewater and lemon rind, and decorated with flower petals. By the mid–1700s cake and biscuits had appeared as a base, softened with sweet wine and topped with an egg custard and whipped cream. They were sometimes decorated with 'shot comfits' (sugar-coated celery seeds or tiny particles of orris root). Candied peel and jam appear in recipes from the 1800s, but things went downhill in the additive-happy 1970s, where all too often trifle meant squelchy jelly, gloopy custard, fake cream and a sprinkling of sugar strands or – worse – glacé cherries and angelica.

That said, there is no definitive recipe for trifle – perhaps that's why I like it so much. It is the ultimate flexible pud. You are free to play around with ingredients, changing the type of cake, fruit and decorations as the mood or season takes you. Many families swear by their own version. The 'trifle' that made its annual appearance on Christmas Eve during my childhood was a particularly loose interpretation: assembled in individual bowls, each contained a couple of slices of Swiss roll soaked in sherry, topped with canned mandarin segments and a dollop of clotted cream. We loved it.

I often make a trifle at Christmas, but it is equally likely to turn up at a dinner party or a summer lunch. Whatever the occasion, it is always greeted enthusiastically by adults and children alike, and there is never any left over. It is also supremely quick and easy, and can be made in advance. Decorate it or not as you please. Toasted flaked almonds, fresh berries or crystallized rose petals all look pretty. Just lay off the angelica.

Summer fruit trifle

A good trifle is sure to be a crowd-pleaser, and once you've enjoyed this summer fruit version, play around a bit. Try using apricot jam and stewed apricots with amaretti biscuits in the base; or fill the sponges with lemon curd with fresh raspberries in between and to decorate; or sandwich chocolate cake with cherry jam, top with cherry compote, then decorate with shavings of dark chocolate.

8 trifle sponges or a plain sponge cake (slightly dry is fine)

a few spoonfuls of fruits of the forest jam (page 25)

150 ml (5 fl oz) sherry, Crème de Cassis or a good-quality fruit cordial

500 g (1 lb 2 oz) mixed summer berries (defrosted if frozen)

500 g (1 lb 2 oz) fresh custard

500 ml (18 fl oz) double or whipping cream

Serves 8–10

1 Cut the trifle sponges in half lengthways, spread thickly with jam and sandwich together. Place in the bottom of a large bowl.

2 Pour the alcohol or cordial over the sponges so that they are well soaked. I like a mixture of sherry and Crème de Cassis, but any kind of sweet wine or spirit will do.

3 Tip the fruits on top of the sponge and squash down a little to release some of the juice. Pour the custard over the fruit.

4 Whip the cream until it is in soft peaks (don't over-whip) and spoon over the custard. If you want to decorate it (I don't usually bother), then do so just before serving.

Linzertorte

Crumbly, nutty dough with a jammy filling, the earliest recipe for this classic Austrian cake dates back to 1653, making it one of the oldest cakes in the world. Raspberry or redcurrant jams are traditional, but others work well too – try blackcurrant or apricot. This is a large and glorious jam tart really.

150 g (5½ oz) sugar

150 g (5½ oz) ground almonds or hazelnuts

2 tsp ground cinnamon

1 tsp ground cloves

finely grated zest of 1 lemon

250 g (9 oz) plain flour

150 g (5½ oz) butter or margarine

1 egg

200 g (7 oz) raspberry jam (page 24)

a dusting of icing sugar, to serve

whipped cream, to serve

Makes 16 slices

1 Preheat the oven to 180°C (350°F). Stir the sugar, nuts, spices and lemon zest together in a mixing bowl, then add the flour.

2 Add the butter and rub in until you have a crumbly mixture the texture of breadcrumbs.

3 Beat the egg in a separate bowl then add to the crumbs and stir in carefully until the dough comes together. Knead briefly in the bowl then chill in the fridge for at least 30 minutes.

4 Grease a loose-bottomed 25 cm (10 in) cake tin. Press two-thirds of the dough into the tin, making it a little higher around the edge. Do this with your fingers as the dough is too crumbly for a rolling pin. Spread the jam over the base.

5 Split the remaining dough into about 10 pieces. Knead each one a little then roll into long strips with your fingers and lay them on the cake in a lattice pattern. Alternatively, press flat and cut into shapes with a biscuit cutter and place over the jam.

6 Bake for 30–40 minutes. This cake tastes better for being left a day or two, if you can wait. Dust with icing sugar and serve with whipped cream.

Jammy rice pudding

This is a stove-top version – creamy and soothing and served with the jam of your choice. Any berry jam is good, or try it with cherry and kirsch jam (page 49). A sprinkling of cinnamon sugar (page 140) on top wouldn't go amiss either. Add a little double cream for an especially rich version.

600 ml (1 pint) full-fat milk

a few drops vanilla extract or vanilla bean paste

1 small cinnamon stick

a strip of lemon peel

115 g (4 oz) pudding or risotto rice

60 g (2¼ oz) sugar

jam, to serve

Serves 4

1 Put the milk, vanilla, cinnamon stick and lemon peel in a saucepan and heat almost to boiling point.

2 Add the rice, bring briefly to the boil then lower the heat and simmer for 30 minutes, stirring from time to time, until the rice has absorbed most of the milk.

3 Remove the lemon peel and cinnamon stick. Add the sugar and stir until dissolved. Simmer for a further 5 minutes until the rice is thoroughly cooked and creamy. Serve warm with a generous helping of jam.

A proper Devonshire cream tea

You will need:

Scones
freshly baked (page 186)

Clotted cream
in liberal quantities

Homemade jam
strawberry for preference
(page 26), with raspberry
a close second (page 24)

A large pot of leaf tea
freshly brewed

My culinary roots are pretty confused. Part of me hankers after goulash, sauerkraut and yeasted cakes filled with poppy seeds and dark plum paste; but I can't escape the fact that my taste buds received their early education in the south west of England, home of the cream tea. 'Give 'em a Gurt Big Dollop' was the 1970s slogan of Devon's dairy marketing board, advertised in huge letters on the sides of double-decker buses urging people to pile on the (clotted) cream.

Clotted cream is made in the West Country and until relatively recently, most of it stayed there, although you could order it by post if you were in the know. Nowadays it is available in many supermarkets, though you can still have it mailed direct from the farm. For me, the best clotted cream must be thick, supremely unctuous, yet grainy, and with a decent crust on top. It has a very high fat content (minimum 55%). Don't let that bother you, though. This is the stuff of treats, not for everyday. If you cannot get hold of clotted cream, use the thickest, unsweetened double cream you can find (whipped cream is not dense enough). Or try beating together one part mascarpone to two parts thick double cream with a tiny bit of icing sugar.

And now to the cream tea: served in any number of cafés and teashops in the UK, all too often it falls short of expectations. The worst and most widely perpetrated crime is to skimp on the amount of jam and cream. The best ones come with mountains of the stuff – a school friend once took me to a teashop on Dartmoor, warning me with delight, 'They challenge you to finish the cream'. If you can find such a place, that's wonderful. But I believe the best cream teas are made at home. Get out your best china. Take the tea with milk. Spread the jam and cream on your scones as generously as you like. The Devonian way is to put the cream on the scone first and the jam on top. The Cornish do it the other way around. Either way, you won't be needing dinner.

Schnitzel

Traditional *Wiener Schnitzel* (Viennese escalope) must, by law, be made from veal. It can be made from pork or chicken, but usually described as 'Viennese-style'. Whichever meat you favour, the traditional accompaniment to a Schnitzel is potato salad and lots of cranberry sauce.

4 escalopes, about 150 g (5½ oz) each – veal, pork, chicken or turkey

40 g (1½ oz) plain flour

salt and pepper

2 eggs, beaten

approx 70 g (2½ oz) dry breadcrumbs

sunflower or other vegetable oil for frying (lard is more traditional, but oil rather healthier)

1 lemon, cut into wedges, to serve

cranberry sauce (page 33), to serve

Serves 4

1 Pound the meat to a thickness of about 6 mm (¼ in) with a meat mallet or rolling pin.

2 You will need three shallow bowls: in the first, put the flour and season it with salt and pepper; in the second, beat the eggs; and place the breadcrumbs in the third.

3 Heat the oil in a deep-sided frying pan. Coat each escalope with the seasoned flour, then dip in the beaten egg, and finally the breadcrumbs. There is no need to press the breadcrumbs into the meat – the coating is not supposed to stick too closely.

4 When the oil is really hot, fry the schnitzels for 4–5 minutes on each side until golden brown. Make sure they don't stick – they should float in the pan.

5 Remove from the pan and drain on kitchen paper.

Serve with lemon wedges and cranberry sauce.

Mushroom, cranberry and pine nut tart

This tart has become something of a tradition in our house as the vegetarian option at Christmas. It goes well with the usual trimmings of a roast dinner. It is also delicious served warm with a green salad and perhaps some buttery mash – and more cranberry sauce, of course!

For the pastry

175 g (6 oz) plain flour

a pinch of salt

85 g (3 oz) butter or margarine (or half butter, half vegetable shortening)

1–2 tbsp cold water

For the filling

30 g (1 oz) butter

1 medium red onion, chopped

1 garlic clove, crushed

500 g (1 lb 2 oz) mushrooms, sliced (use a mixture, such as button, chestnut, Portobello)

55 g (2 oz) pine nuts

40 g (1½ oz) fresh breadcrumbs (white or brown)

60 g (2¼ oz) cranberry sauce (page 33)

2 tbsp double cream

salt and pepper

Serves 6

1 Preheat the oven to 190°C (375°F). Make the pastry: sift the flour and salt together in a mixing bowl. Rub in the butter or margarine until it resembles fine breadcrumbs. Sprinkle a little cold water over and stir with a knife until the pastry starts to come together. Use your fingers to pull it together into a ball, adding extra water a tiny bit at a time if necessary. Wrap in cling film and chill for 30 minutes.

2 Roll out the pastry on a floured surface and transfer it to a lightly greased 26 cm (10 in) tart dish or tin. Prick the base with a fork and bake blind for 20–25 minutes until just cooked.

3 Meanwhile make the filling. Melt the butter in a large, heavy-bottomed saucepan and fry the onion and garlic until soft. Add the mushrooms and cook for a further 4–5 minutes.

4 Toast the pine nuts in a dry pan over a high heat for a couple of minutes; shake from time to time.

5 Add the breadcrumbs, most of the pine nuts, about ⅓ of the cranberry sauce and the cream to the mushroom mixture and stir together. Season and cook for a minute or two more.

6 Spread the remaining cranberry sauce on the cooked pastry base. Pile in the mushroom filling and return to the oven for 5 minutes. Scatter the remaining pine nuts over the tart before serving.

Queen of puddings

With its custardy base, jammy centre and fluffy meringue topping, this is a rather whimsical pudding – sweet, comforting and pretty. Based on a 17th-century recipe, it was originally created by chefs at Buckingham Palace for Queen Victoria.

For the base

600 ml (1 pint) full-fat milk

125 g (4½ oz) fresh white breadcrumbs

25 g (1 oz) caster sugar

4 egg yolks

finely grated zest of 1 lemon

150–200 g (5½–7 oz) raspberry jam (enough to cover the base), page 24

For the meringue

4 egg whites

100 g (3½ oz) caster sugar

Serves 6–8

1 Preheat the oven to 180°C (350°F). Heat the milk until it is almost at boiling point. Remove from heat and stir in the breadcrumbs. Leave to absorb for 10–15 minutes.

2 Add the sugar, egg yolks and lemon zest and beat together. Pour the mixture into a 1.2 litre (2 pint) buttered ovenproof dish and bake for 25–30 minutes or until just set in the middle.

3 Gently warm the jam until runny (a few seconds in the microwave should do it) and spread over the cooked base.

4 Whisk the egg whites to soft peaks. Whisk in half the sugar, then fold in the rest with a metal spoon. Spoon the meringue over the jam.

5 Bake the pudding for a further 10–15 minutes until the meringue is lightly browned and starting to crisp. Serve warm.

Juicy

Plums, greengages, apricots
and cherries

Plum and mulled wine jam

'The house smells like Christmas!' commented James, wandering into the kitchen while this jam was cooking. He's right, and for that reason I prefer to make this once the weather turns cooler. Plums are the ideal match for warming winter spices.

1.6 kg (3 lb 8 oz) plums, halved and stoned

350 ml (12 fl oz) red wine (cheap but drinkable)

1 mulled wine spice bag, plus 2 pieces cinnamon bark and a few cloves tied in a piece of muslin

a pinch of ground allspice

grated zest and juice of 1 orange

juice of ½ lemon

1.6 kg (3 lb 8 oz) granulated sugar

Makes 6–7 x 340 g (12 oz) jars

Keeps for 12 months

1 Put the plums, wine, spices, orange zest, orange juice and lemon juice in a preserving pan. Cook over a low heat for about 20 minutes, or until the plums are really soft. Once the sugar is added, the softening process is halted, and tough fruit skins will spoil the preserve.

2 Remove the spices and add the sugar, stirring until completely dissolved. Bring to the boil and cook at a full rolling boil for 8–10 minutes. Test for a set then pot into hot sterilized jars (page 18).

TIP

I sometimes make this with frozen plums. Do not defrost before cooking as they will go dark and mushy – just cook until soft.

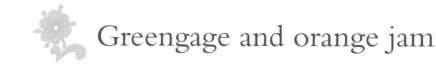

Greengage and orange jam

Our greengage tree is often so prolific that I am always looking for new ways to cook with them. On their own or with a single spice (star anise, vanilla or cinnamon), greengage jam is one of my very favourite things to spread on crumpets or toast. The addition of freshly squeezed orange juice and zest makes this a perfect breakfast preserve. If you can't find greengages, use plums instead.

1.3 kg (3 lb) greengages, halved and stoned

300 ml (10 fl oz) water

zest and freshly squeezed juice of 3 oranges

1.3 kg (3 lb) granulated sugar

a knob of butter

Makes 6–7 x 340 g (12 oz) jars

Keeps for 12 months

1 Put the greengages in a preserving pan with the water and orange juice and zest, and cook gently for about 30 minutes, until the skins are very soft.

2 Take the pan off the heat and add the sugar, stirring until dissolved. Add the butter and stir it in.

3 Return to the heat and bring to the boil. Cook at a full rolling boil for 10–15 minutes, stirring frequently, then test for a set (page 18). When ready pot into hot sterilized jars (page 18).

Apricot jam

This recipe comes originally from Brno in the Czech Republic from our Tante Hanne, who made fantastic preserves. Breakfast at her house was a memorable affair: aromatic coffee, fresh rolls and her wonderful homemade jam. This is a recipe in two stages: the prepared fruit is macerated in the sugar overnight and the jam is cooked the next day.

1.6 kg (3 lb 8 oz) apricots, stoned and quartered

1 kg (2 lb 4 oz) granulated sugar: 600–700 g (1 lb 5 oz–1 lb 9 oz) per 1 kg of stoned fruit

juice of ½ lemon (optional)

a knob of butter

Makes 6–7 x 340 g (12 oz) jars

Keeps for 12 months

1 Put the apricots and sugar into a large bowl and stir well. Cover with a clean cloth and leave overnight to allow the sugar to work its magic and the apricots to release their juice.

2 The next day, tip the mixture into a preserving pan and add the lemon juice. Bring to the boil, then lower the heat. It foams a lot but adding the butter at this stage helps to disperse scum.

3 Cook over a low heat for 30–45 minutes, stirring frequently. Test for a set (page 18): it should be thick but will be soft set. Pot into hot sterilized jars (page 18).

Cherry and kirsch jam

Stoning cherries is a fiddly, hand-staining process. Use a cherry-stoner to speed things up, or cook them whole and remove the stones with a slotted spoon later on. Alternatively, cheat and use frozen, ready pitted ones. Cherries are low in pectin so they make a soft-set jam, perfect on crusty bread or in puddings.

1 kg (2 lb 4 oz) cherries

juice of 2–3 lemons

50 ml (2 fl oz) water

750 g–1 kg (1 lb 10 oz–2 lb 4 oz) sugar, depending on the sweetness of the cherries

a knob of butter

60 ml (2¼ fl oz) kirsch or brandy (optional)

Makes 4 x 340 g (12 oz) jars

Keeps for 12 months

1 Put the cherries, lemon juice and water in a preserving pan and cook gently for 15–20 minutes, stirring now and then, until very soft.

2 Remove from the heat, stir in the sugar until dissolved, then add the butter. Return to the heat and bring to the boil. Cook at a full rolling boil for 15–20 minutes, stirring occasionally. Test for a set (page 18).

3 Once setting point has been reached, stir in the kirsch or brandy and leave to stand for 15 minutes before potting (page 18). Omit the alcohol if you prefer, or add a couple of teaspoons to individual jars once filled (stir in with a teaspoon handle).

Chinese plum sauce

This sauce is one of my favourite uses for plums. It's great with oriental snacks or crispy duck, and a useful cooking ingredient too (add a spoonful to stir-fries). It is not essential to make it in one go – the cooked plum mixture will happily wait before the puréeing stage. Likewise, once you have puréed you can leave that mixture for a few hours before completing the process.

2 kg (4 lb 8 oz) plums, halved and stoned

2 large onions, chopped

6 large garlic cloves, chopped

200 g (7 oz) fresh root ginger, chopped

1 medium hot red chilli, chopped (no need to de-seed)

1 litre (1¾ pints) rice wine vinegar (or red wine vinegar)

200 ml (7 fl oz) soy sauce (light or dark)

1 tsp ground ginger

4–5 star anise

2–3 cm (1 in) cinnamon bark

1 tsp Sichuan pepper

700 g (1 lb 9 oz) light muscovado sugar

Makes 8 x 340 g (12 oz) jars

Keeps for 12 months

1 Put the plums, onions, garlic, root ginger, chilli, vinegar and soy sauce in a preserving pan and slowly bring to the boil. Cover and simmer for 20–30 minutes until everything is soft.

2 Push the mixture through a sieve or mouli and return the purée to the cleaned pan. Crush the spices in a pestle and mortar and tie them together in a piece of muslin. Add the spice bag (or ground spices) and sugar to the pan and stir well.

3 Bring the mixture to the boil, stirring frequently. Reduce the heat and simmer for about an hour until the sauce is thick and well reduced. Remove the spice bag and pour the sauce into hot sterilized bottles or jars (page 18).

VARIATION

Try alternative spices, such as 2 tsps Chinese five-spice powder and ½ tsp ground cinnamon.

Spicy fruit ketchup

This is a good recipe for using up a glut of fruit – mix and match with whatever you have. It is perfect served with an English breakfast or sausages and mash. Try it in a bacon sandwich: floury white bread, generously buttered, a slathering of spicy fruit ketchup, salty bacon fried until crisp, maybe a slice or two of tomato…heaven.

1 hot dried chilli
(or more if you like)

2 tsp coriander seeds

2 tsp allspice berries

1 tsp black peppercorns

a few cloves

2.5 kg (5 lb 8 oz) fruit (a mixture of plums, greengages and apples)

300 g (10½ oz) mixed dried fruit (raisins, currants, sultanas, dates, prunes – whatever you have in the store cupboard)

500 g (1 lb 2 oz) onions, chopped

60 g (2¼ oz) fresh root ginger, peeled and chopped

1.2 litres (2 pints) vinegar (distilled malt or wine vinegar)

500 g (1 lb 2 oz) demerara sugar

100 g (3½ oz) dark muscovado sugar

1 tbsp salt

Makes 7 x 340 g (12 oz) jars

Keeps for 12–18 months

1 Tie all the spices in a piece of muslin or put them into a spice ball. Stone and halve the plums and gages; core and roughly chop the apples (no need to peel).

2 Put all the fruit, dried fruit, onions, ginger, spices and 700 ml (1¼ pints) of the vinegar in a preserving pan and slowly bring to the boil. Simmer until the fruit is very soft, about 30 minutes, stirring occasionally.

3 Remove the spice bag and push the mixture through a sieve or a mouli. Put the purée in the cleaned pan with the sugars, salt and remaning vinegar, and stir well.

4 Bring the mixture to the boil, then reduce the heat and simmer for 45 minutes to 1 hour, stirring frequently, until you have a thick, smooth pouring sauce. Pot into hot sterilized bottles or jars (page 18).

VARIATIONS

Plums make a great base for this sauce, but you can use tomatoes instead. Add a handful of blackberries or damsons.

Turn up the heat with extra chillies (fresh, if you prefer), or try adding mustard seeds, ground nutmeg, ground ginger or some chopped garlic.

Greengage, apple and walnut chutney

Some chutneys need hours of slow cooking, while others are altogether speedier. This is one of the latter and has a special place in my heart as it is the first chutney I ever made. Great with anything cheesy, it is fresh-tasting with the walnuts supplying a pleasing bite. You can use any apple variety, but I favour something tart and crunchy, like a Granny Smith.

1 kg (2 lb 4 oz) greengages

4 eating apples

100 g (3½ oz) walnuts

300 g (10½ oz) granulated sugar

300 ml (10 fl oz) cider vinegar or white wine vinegar

1 large onion, chopped

zest and juice of 2 oranges

2 tsp mixed spice

a pinch of salt

Makes 4 x 340 g (12 oz) jars

Keeps for 12 months

1 Stone and halve the greengages; peel, core and roughly chop the apples; and roughly chop the walnuts.

2 Put the sugar, vinegar, onion, orange juice and zest, spice and salt in a large pan and heat gently, stirring, until the sugar has dissolved. Bring to the boil and simmer for 10 minutes.

3 Add the greengages and apples and cook until the fruit is soft and the liquid well reduced (about 30–45 minutes). Stir in the walnuts and cook for a minute or two more, then pot into hot sterilized jars (page 18).

Kaiserschmarren *(Emperor's pancake)*

One of many legends about this classic Austrian dish is that Emperor Franz Josef's cook once had a disaster when cooking pancakes. The emperor exclaimed, 'What kind of a "Schmarrn" is this?' (*'schmarrn'* means 'a mess' in Austrian German). He must have liked it, though, for the dish became hugely popular. And it's a lot quicker than making a stack of pancakes.

250 ml (9 fl oz) milk

150 g (5½ oz) plain flour

a pinch of salt

30 g (1 oz) sugar

4 eggs

60 g (2¼ oz) raisins (optional)

a generous knob of butter

a dusting of icing sugar, to serve

jam or fruit compote, to serve

Serves 4

1 Whisk the milk, flour, salt and sugar together in a large bowl. Separate the eggs and whisk the yolks into the batter.

2 In a separate bowl, whisk the egg whites to stiff peaks and fold into the batter. If using raisins, fold them in gently at this stage.

3 Heat the butter in a large frying pan and pour in the batter. Cook until golden-brown underneath (about 4 minutes) – the upper side should still be a bit runny. To turn the pancake over, I find the easiest way is to cut it into quarters and turn one at a time. Cook for a few more minutes and then tear the pancake into pieces (use 2 forks for this). Fry for a further minute or two until cooked through.

4 Dust generously with sifted icing sugar and serve with the jam or compote of your choice. Traditional accompaniments are plum compote, stewed apple or cranberry sauce – I like it with a plum or apricot jam.

VARIATION

Serve with sliced bananas and cinnamon sugar; or slice bananas into the unset batter while cooking.

Plum crumble cake

This recipe is the perfect way to use up a crop of plums. It is widely enjoyed in central Europe, where it is often made with a yeast base, but this recreates my mother's version, which is somewhere between a sponge cake and a crumble. It also works well with apricots, apples or rhubarb.

For the topping

115 g (4 oz) margarine or butter

140 g (5 oz) flour
(self-raising or plain)

115 g (4 oz) granulated sugar

For the base

150 g (5½ oz) margarine or butter

150 g (5½ oz) sugar

2 eggs

150 g (5½ oz) self-raising flour

2 tsp milk

Fruit

500 g (1 lb 2 oz) plums,
stoned and halved

Makes about 12 slices

Keep for 2–3 days
(but three hungry boys can polish
it off in the space of an hour)

1 Preheat the oven to 180°C (350°F) and grease and line a 20 cm (8 in) square cake tin with baking parchment.

2 Make the crumble topping: rub the butter into the flour with your fingers until it resembles coarse, sticky breadcrumbs, then stir in the sugar.

3 In a separate bowl, make the sponge base: cream the margarine or butter and sugar together, then beat in the eggs. Stir in the flour, then add the milk and beat well.

4 Spread the sponge mixture into the cake tin. Place the plum halves on top of the base, on their sides or cut side up, crowding them closely together. Finally scatter the crumble mixture over the plums. Bake for 45 minutes to 1 hour. Leave to cool in the tin before serving.

VARIATION

Add a pinch of mixed spice, cinnamon or ginger to the crumble topping.

Crunchy

Apples, pears and rhubarb

All about apples

Empire, Cox's Orange Pippin, Russet, Worcester Pearmain, Bramley's Seedling, Honeycrisp, Jazz, Discovery, Beauty of Bath, Scrumptious, Chivers Delight… Just a few of the enchantingly named apple varieties now in existence. Apples were cultivated and introduced to much of Europe by the Romans. European settlers in turn took apples to the Americas, and today they are a truly global fruit, grown everywhere from China to Chile.

Straight from the fruit bowl or as an ingredient, apples are surely one of our most versatile fruits. Eat raw in salads, grate them into muesli, or add apple slices to a cheese sandwich. Pectin-rich and pleasingly tart, cooking apples make an excellent base for savoury and sweet jellies (pages 123 and 154). Pies, tarts and crumbles would be lost without them; and they are a natural partner for pork and other rich meats, as a sauce or simply pan-fried in slices.

Apples make fine drinks too. As a child, I looked forward to trips to Germany when I would be offered as much apple juice as I wanted – back then it was not widely available in England. Happily, freshly pressed juices, as well as cartons of clear juice for everyday, now line supermarket shelves. Cider is enjoying a revival too, and many countries have their own styles of the glorious stuff. And let's not forget cider vinegar: one of the oldest folk remedies around, its virtues were extolled in one of my mother's favourite books, *Folk Medicine: A Vermont Doctor's Guide to Good Health*. From sore throats to arthritis, there's a chance that cider vinegar can help.

I think you're getting the picture: apples taste great, and they are good for you – as the saying goes, 'An apple a day keeps the doctor away'. I'm not sure if apple crumble counts, but it's a risk I am prepared to take.

Apple crumble

A fruit crumble is the British pud at its simplest and best. Stuck for weekend lunch ideas, my fallback is a hearty soup with bread and cheese and a big dish of crumble to follow. Bramleys are my first choice, usually with a handful of blackberries to add colour and flavour.

For the crumble

225 g (8 oz) flour
(plain or self-raising, either will do)

140 g (5 oz) granulated sugar

140 g (5 oz) butter or margarine
(not too soft)

For the fruit filling

3 large cooking apples, about 830 g
(1lb 13 oz) unprepared weight

a handful of blackberries (optional)

a squeeze of lemon juice (optional)

60–90 g (2¼–3¼ oz) sugar,
depending on the tartness of
the fruit

a pinch of ground spice (cinnamon,
mixed spice or ginger)

Serves 6

1 Preheat the oven to 180°C (350°F). Make the crumble: stir the flour and sugar together. Cut in the butter using a knife, then rub together with your fingers until you have a crumbly mixture.

2 Peel and core the apples and cut into smallish pieces. Place in a 2 litre (3½ pint) ovenproof dish (with the blackberries if you are using them), squeeze the lemon juice over and stir in the sugar and spice.

3 Scatter the crumble mixture evenly on top and bake in the oven for approximately 40–50 minutes. Serve with custard, vanilla ice cream or thick pouring cream.

VARIATION

Substitute rolled oats for part of the flour (3 parts flour to 1 part oats). Sometimes I put spice in the crumble topping, sometimes in the fruit – occasionally in both.

Ann's apple chutney

My godmother Ann's apple chutney was legendary in our house and cheered up many a cheese sandwich. She made it with Charles Ross apples from her tree, and kept us well supplied. Mild and fruity, it is also excellent with cold meats.

900 g (2 lb) apples
(prepared weight)

700 g (1 lb 9 oz) granulated sugar

2 tsp salt

2 tsp ground ginger

a large pinch of mixed spice

450 g (1 lb) raisins

2 medium onions, chopped
(optional)

1.2 litres (2 pints) wine vinegar

**Makes about 6 x 340 g
(12 oz) jars**

Keeps for 12 months

1 Core, peel and chop the apples. Put them, together with the sugar, salt, spices and raisins (and onions, if using) in a large pan with half the vinegar and bring to the boil very slowly, stirring to dissolve the sugar. Stir frequently when the apples begin to soften.

2 When all is soft (after about 15–20 minutes) add the rest of the vinegar and boil for about 30 minutes more, stirring frequently, until it is well reduced. Draw a wooden spoon across the surface – if it leaves a trail, the chutney is ready. Pot into hot sterilized jars (page 18).

VARIATION

For a spicier version, add a pinch of chilli flakes and/or a piece of finely chopped fresh root ginger.

Pear and ginger jam

When I was young we had three pear trees in our small garden in Devon – one survives and produces a fine crop of large, juicy soft-skinned fruit. Each autumn I go to collect them, keep the best ones for eating, and spend hours peeling and chopping the rest to be frozen and used in jams, chutneys and desserts. Then, my suitcase full of treasure, I catch the train back to London.

1.3 kg (3 lb) pears
(prepared weight)

225 g (8 oz) preserved ginger

1.1 kg (2 lb 8 oz) granulated sugar

1 tsp ground cinnamon

grated rind of 2 lemons

Makes 7 x 340 g (12 oz) jars

Keeps for 12 months

1 Core and slice the pears. Peel any with tough skin. Chop the ginger.

2 Put all the ingredients in a preserving pan and bring slowly to the boil, stirring well to dissolve the sugar.

3 Boil for about 10 minutes, stirring occasionally to prevent sticking, until setting point is reached. Pears are low in pectin, so this is a soft jam – it will thicken rather than gel, but should not be too runny. Test for a set and pot into hot sterilized jars (page 18) when ready.

VARIATION

This jam can also be made with cooking apples, or a mixture of apples and pears.

This was one of my mother's favourite recipes. Her notes read: 'Based on a recipe from *The Good Cook's Encyclopedia*, bought for me by your father on our first trip to Plymouth in 1961 at a bookshop inside the railway station. Price Two Shillings and Elevenpence – roughly 15p at today's price. I used *Langenscheidts Taschenwörterbuch* (pocket dictionary) for translation.'

Pear and chocolate jam

An abundance of pears one year led me to experiment. This recipe was definitely a hit, especially with Alexander – pear jam with very dark, intense chocolate stirred into it. It has a particular affinity with buttery things, such as brioches and croissants, and is great as a filling for pancakes, especially with vanilla ice cream.

1 kg (2 lb 4 oz) ripe pears

juice of 2 lemons

800 g (1 lb 12 oz) granulated sugar

a pinch of ground cinnamon

150 g (5½ oz) good-quality dark chocolate (minimum 70% cocoa solids)

Makes 6–7 x 227 g (8 oz) jars

Keeps for 12 months

1 Peel, core and dice the pears; roughly chop the chocolate.

2 Put the pears and lemon juice in a preserving pan with a splash of water and cook over a gentle heat for 4–5 minutes, stirring from time to time.

3 Add the sugar and cinnamon and stir over a low heat until the sugar has dissolved. Simmer for

20–30 minutes then test for a set (page 18). It will be a soft consistency, but should not be too liquid.

4 Stir the chocolate into the warm jam until it is melted and thoroughly combined. Pot into hot sterilized jars (page 18).

Speedy pear and chocolate tart

My friend Deborah made this with a jar of pear and chocolate jam. I think it's a rather fabulous idea.

4 firm pears

300 ml (10 fl oz) water

a squeeze of lemon juice

1 tbsp sugar

a jar pear and chocolate jam

a pastry case, baked blind (bought or homemade)

1 Peel, core and halve the pears. Lightly poach them in the water, lemon juice and sugar.

2 Spread the jam on the pastry case and lay the poached pears attractively on top

Serve with plenty of crème fraîche.

Sybille's rhubarb and apricot jam *infused with Earl Grey tea*

Pink and green rhubarb combined with orange apricots make this a rather pretty, multi-coloured preserve, and the Earl Grey tea adds a subtle flavour. The apricots provide sweetness so the sugar content is lower than in other jams.

200 g (7 oz) dried apricots

2 tsp loose-leaf Earl Grey tea (or 2 teabags)

300 ml (10 fl oz) boiling water

1 kg (2 lb 3 oz) rhubarb

juice of ½ lemon

500 g (1 lb 2 oz) jam sugar with pectin

Makes 4–5 x 340 g (12 oz) jars

Keeps for 12 months

1 Quarter the apricots (use ordinary dried apricots, not the very soft 'ready-to-eat' variety) and put them in a heatproof bowl.

2 Make a pot of strong Earl Grey tea: 2 teaspoons of loose-leaf tea, or 2 teabags, with the boiling water. Pour the tea over the apricots, give them a good stir, and leave to soak overnight. If you're not keen on the tea idea, simply soak the apricots in boiling water.

3 Wash the rhubarb if necessary and cut into 2 cm (¾ in) pieces. Place the rhubarb, apricots (plus soaking liquid) and lemon juice in a preserving pan. Cook over a low heat, stirring frequently, until the rhubarb is soft and mushy (about 10–15 minutes).

4 Take the pan off the heat, add the sugar and stir until dissolved. Return to the heat and bring to the boil. Cook for about 3–5 minutes, stirring now and then. Test for a set and pot into hot sterilized jars (page 18).

Rhubarb chutney

with orange, ginger and cardamom

This recipe started as a very basic rhubarb chutney, but I kept having ideas about new ingredients to add. Here is the result: a fresh yet mellow chutney to enjoy with cheese, cold meats and pâtés. It disappears fast in my house. Dates make a good substitute for the raisins.

3 small red onions, chopped

300 ml (10 fl oz) white wine vinegar

5 cm (2 in) piece of fresh root ginger, finely chopped

1 tsp ground ginger

150 g (5½ oz) raisins

a pinch of ground cinnamon

seeds from 12 cardamom pods, lightly crushed in a pestle and mortar

1 kg (2 lb 4 oz) rhubarb, cut into 2 cm (¾ in) pieces

zest and juice of 2 oranges

400 g (14 oz) granulated sugar

Makes 6–7 x 340 g (12 oz) jars

Keeps for 12 months

1 Put the onions, vinegar, fresh root ginger, raisins and spices in a preserving pan, bring to the boil then turn off the heat and leave to infuse for at least 10 minutes. This gives you time to cut up the rhubarb (kitchen scissors make light work of this) and prepare the oranges.

2 Add the rhubarb, sugar, orange zest and juice to the pan. Bring slowly to the boil, stirring until the sugar has dissolved. Simmer gently for 30 minutes, stirring from time to time. It will be a soft consistency but should not be too liquid. Pot into hot sterilized jars (page 18).

Ideally leave it for a few weeks to mature. I can rarely wait that long.

Potato, pear and blue cheese gratin

My friend Julia gave me the idea for this recipe on my return from Devon with the annual pear harvest. Most gratin recipes require you to peel the potatoes, but red-skinned Desirees are too good-looking to mess with. And a little extra fibre is no bad thing in such a rich dish. Serve with a peppery watercress salad and bramble jelly (page 154).

750 g (1 lb 10 oz) Desiree potatoes

3 pears (ripe but firm)

150 g (5½ oz) blue cheese (Stilton, Saint Agur, Dolcelatte), cut into cubes

1 fat garlic clove, sliced

salt and pepper

300 ml (10 fl oz) double cream

200 ml (7 fl oz) full-fat milk

Serves 4 as a main dish or 6 as a side dish

1 Preheat the oven to 160°C (320°F). Butter a large baking dish.

2 Scrub the potatoes (do not peel) and slice thinly, about 3 mm (⅛ in) thick. Cut the pears into quarters (again, no need to peel), core and slice each quarter lengthways (a bit thicker than the potatoes).

3 Layer the potatoes, pears, blue cheese and garlic in the dish, seasoning with salt and pepper as you go. Mix the cream and milk together in a jug and pour it over.

4 Bake for 1–1¼ hours until the potatoes are golden and well cooked. Leave to stand for a few minutes before serving.

Tangy

Oranges, lemons and limes

Marmalade

'Paddington was a great believer in marmalade. He'd often used it for all sorts of things besides eating, and now that he took a closer look at Mr Curry's saw, he felt sure it might come in very useful for greasing the blade in an emergency.'

Michael Bond, *Paddington at Large*

I recommend that you eat your marmalade rather than use it as a substitute for WD-40, but don't limit it to breakfast time – it makes a great ingredient in cakes and puddings, and is fantastic in savoury dishes too, in a bitter orange sauce to accompany duck, for example, or to glaze a baked ham. The marmalade recipes in this chapter make a good-sized batch so there will be plenty to spread on your toast, with a jar or two to spare for a marmalade and carrot cake (page 84).

You can make marmalade from any citrus fruits, but marmalade-lovers favour tangy Sevilles, sometimes known as bitter oranges. With their rough skin, numerous pips and tart flesh they are not, on the face of it, terribly attractive, but cook them up with sugar and water and these ugly sisters are magically transformed. They are available only for a few weeks in January and February and not always easy to find, an elusiveness that for me adds to their appeal. If you don't have time to make marmalade during their short season, they freeze well. Wash, freeze whole and defrost at room temperature before using. (Freezing reduces the pectin levels, so add the juice of an extra lemon.)

I am a relative novice when it comes to making marmalade: my first attempt wasn't bad, but rather labour-intensive. Since then I have experimented with various methods until arriving at a Seville orange marmalade recipe (page 76) that produces good results without being too fiddly. And nothing cheers a January day like the bitter-sweet fragrance of oranges simmering away in the kitchen.

Seville orange marmalade

This is a good, everyday homely preserve, delicious and relatively simple, which knocks spots off shop-bought marmalade. White granulated sugar produces a clearer, lighter-coloured marmalade, demerara sugar gives a darker, deeper-flavoured result, while light muscovado adds hints of caramel. If you can't decide, a mixture of one part demerara to two parts white sugar works well.

750–800 g (1 lb 10 oz–1lb 12 oz) Seville oranges (about 6)

2 litres (3½ pints) water

50 ml (2 fl oz) freshly squeezed lemon juice (from about 1½– 2 lemons)

1.5 kg (3 lb 5 oz) sugar

Makes about 7 x 340 g (12 oz) jars

Keeps for 2 years

1 Wash the oranges thoroughly and put the whole fruit into a preserving pan with the water. Squeeze the lemons, set the juice aside and add the lemon shells to the pan. Bring to the boil and simmer, covered, for about 2 hours. It is essential to cook the fruit until the skins are thoroughly tender – they won't soften any further once sugar is added.

2 Leave to cool (overnight if you wish). Remove the oranges and put them in a colander over the pan. Squash them down a bit with a spoon to extract as much of the pectin-rich liquid as possible.

3 Measure the remaining liquid – you need about 1.1 litres (just under 2 pints) so top up with more water if necessary. Halve the oranges, scoop out the pith and pips from the centres and put these in a sieve over a bowl as you go along. Slice the orange peel and flesh into shreds, as thick or thin as you like. I sometimes shred the lemon peel too.

4 Add all the shredded peel and flesh to the cooking liquid, plus any juice that has dripped from the pips.

5 Add the sugar and reserved lemon juice and set the pan over a low heat, stirring until the sugar is completely dissolved. Bring to the boil and boil rapidly until setting point is reached (page 18). This can take between 15 and 40 minutes, so test for a set after 15 minutes. If it is not ready, boil again, testing at 5 minute intervals.

6 Once setting point is reached, leave to cool for 15–20 minutes, then stir to distribute the peel and pot into hot sterilized jars (page 18).

TIP

If you are a serious marmalade addict, this recipe works well doubled (it just about fits in a preserving pan), but setting time is likely to be nearer 40 minutes.

Lime marmalade

Hot toast with melting butter. A generous spoonful of this fragrant marmalade. A pot of freshly brewed tea or coffee and the Sunday papers. Now that's a pretty fine way to do breakfast. Limes have tough skin so be sure to cook them until the peel is really soft before adding the sugar.

600 g (1 lb 5 oz) ripe juicy limes
(about 6–8)

1.4 litres (2½ pints) boiling water

4 dried Kaffir lime leaves

1 stalk lemon grass

1.3 kg (3 lb) sugar

**Makes about 6–7 x 340 g
(12 oz) jars**

Keeps for 12 months

1 Wash the limes well in warm water. Cut the limes in half lengthwise and slice them as thinly as possible (a very sharp knife helps), discarding the hard ends and any pips as you go.

2 Place the lime slices in a bowl, add the lime leaves and lemon grass, then pour the boiling water over them. Cover with a clean cloth and leave for a few hours or overnight.

3 Fish out the lime leaves and lemon grass and discard, then tip the contents of the bowl into a preserving pan. Bring to the boil then simmer, covered, for about 1–1½ hours until the peel is utterly soft.

4 Remove from the heat, add the sugar and stir until it is dissolved. Then bring back to the boil and cook at a full rolling boil for 6–10 minutes. Test for a set and pot into hot sterilized jars (page 18).

Three-fruit marmalade

This is a marmalade you can make all year round. There is a lot of preparation involved but it's worth it – just choose a time when you have a few hours to spare. You do need a large pan for this recipe: it's a big one and the marmalade foams up a lot during cooking. If you prefer, halve the ingredients, but in this case the setting time may be shorter (10–15 minutes).

4 large lemons

3 large sweet oranges

2 pink or ruby red grapefruit

3.4 litres (6 pints) water

2.7 kg (6 lb) sugar

Makes about 11–12 x 340 g (12 oz) jars

Keeps for 12 months

1 Scrub the fruit well in warm water. Squeeze the lemons and reserve the juice. Peel the oranges and grapefruit and scrape away any thick white pith from the fruit. Cut excess pith from the peel using a sharp knife.

2 Chop the grapefruit and orange flesh into small chunks. Shred the orange, grapefruit and lemon peel (use sharp kitchen scissors). I shred the peel quite finely in this recipe.

3 Put all the chopped fruit, juice and peel in a large preserving pan with the water. Bring to the boil then simmer, covered, for about 1½–2 hours or until the peel is soft (you should be able to crush it easily with your fingers).

4 Add the sugar and stir until dissolved. Bring slowly to the boil, stirring frequently, then cook at a full rolling boil for 20–30 minutes. Test for a set (page 18) and then leave to stand for 10–15 minutes before potting into hot sterilized jars (page 18).

TIP

Turn it into a four-fruit (or even a five-fruit) marmalade: substitute two limes for one of the grapefruit, two tangerines for one orange.

Clementine and passion fruit jelly

Passion fruit seeds look very attractive suspended in this orange jelly. This is another great breakfast preserve, and is delicious on crumpets too. Passion fruit are ripe when they are crinkled and look, well, past it. They taste good with all manner of fruit – strawberries, peaches, mangoes... and orangey things.

1 kg (2 lb 4 oz) clementines

2 lemons

2 litres (3½ pints) water

600–700 g (1 lb 5–1 lb 9 oz) sugar

3 passion fruit

Makes 3–4 x 227 g (8 oz) jars

Keeps for 12 months

1 Chop the clementines and lemons roughly – peel and all. Put them in a preserving pan with the water. Bring to the boil, then cover and simmer for about an hour until the fruit is very soft.

2 Pour the mixture into a scalded jelly bag (page 12) and leave it to drip through overnight.

3 Measure the resulting liquid: for each 400 ml (14 fl oz) juice add 300 g (10½ oz) sugar. Put the liquid and sugar in the pan and heat slowly, stirring. When all the sugar has dissolved, bring to the boil and boil rapidly for 10–15 minutes, or until setting point is reached (page 18).

4 Scoop the pulp and juice from the passion fruit. Stir gently into the jelly and leave for 20 minutes before potting into hot sterilized jars (page 18). If necessary, tip the jars occasionally as it cools to distribute the passion fruit seeds.

Marmalade and carrot cake

I found this in the recipe notebook that I started in my early teens. Although it is written out in my own handwriting I have no idea where it came from, but have happily adopted this foundling nonetheless. Dense, moist and not too sweet, it is a bit grander than the average carrot cake. It's a large one, good for a crowd, and perfect for a winter teatime.

175 g (6 oz) soft brown sugar

175 g (6 oz) margarine

3 eggs, separated

60 g (2½ oz) ground almonds

4 tbsp marmalade, warmed

175 g (6 oz) self-raising flour

175 g (6 oz) carrots, peeled and grated (about 2 medium)

115 g (4 oz) chopped almonds

For the topping

175 g (6 oz) mascarpone

3 tbsp lemon curd

a few strands of orange zest, to decorate

Serves 15 generously

1 Preheat the oven to 180°C (350°F). Grease and line a loose-bottomed 25 cm (10 in) cake tin.

2 Cream the sugar and margarine, then beat in the egg yolks and ground almonds. Add the marmalade, flour, carrots and chopped almonds and mix well.

3 Whisk the egg whites until stiff and fold into the cake mixture. Tip into the prepared tin, level the top, and bake for 40–50 minutes. Leave to cool for 10 minutes before removing from the tin.

4 When the cake has cooled completely, beat the mascarpone and lemon curd together and spread over the cake. Decorate with the orange zest.

Fruit curds

There is a bowl of juicy lemons in the kitchen. Some unsalted butter in the fridge. A bag of sugar in the cupboard. A box of eggs. All that is required from you now is a little time – half an hour should do it – and your undivided attention, and those four everyday ingredients can be transformed into a few magical jars of tart, creamy lemon curd. Your homemade version will be nothing like most shop-bought ones, those glow-in-the-dark gelatinous types, with more than a whiff of floor cleaner about them. I am being a little unfair, for there are some very fine artisan-made curds out there. But the preserve made in your kitchen will be lemon curd at its very best: pale, unctuous, with the odd fleck of zest and a tangy citrus kick. And you will have something truly gorgeous for toast and scones, for filling tarts and for making Karin's fabulous lemon curd cake (page 91). Your friends will be impressed. And – cook's perks – you get to lick the spoon.

Lemon curd is the most well known and popular variety, but all members of the citrus family are good candidates: orange, grapefruit and lime. Other tart fruits also lend themselves well: passion fruit, raspberries and gooseberries all make delicious curds in good-looking pastel shades. Use them to create instant desserts: fill pancakes, fold into whipped cream, top a steamed pudding or ripple into ice cream.

Curd has a reputation for being tricky to make. In fact, it is not only easy, but surprisingly quick. There is one main pitfall, as the similarity of the words 'curd' and 'curdle' might suggest, but don't let that put you off. The trick is to keep whisking, and stop cooking as soon as the curd is thick enough to coat the back of a spoon, before it scrambles. The other thing to bear in mind is that curds need to be refrigerated and eaten within a few weeks, which is rarely a problem in our household.

There's a saying: 'When life throws you a lemon, make lemonade.' And when it throws you three, make lemon curd.

Lemon curd

Spread it on what you will, bake with it or stir into thick yogurt or cream for an instant dessert. The lemons should be ripe and juicy. Keep them at room temperature or warmer — you will get more juice that way. If your lemons are waxed, give them a good scrub in warm water and dry them well.

3 ripe lemons, unwaxed

250 g (9 oz) granulated sugar

125 g (4½ oz) unsalted butter, cut into cubes

3 medium eggs

Makes about 3 x 227 g (8 oz) jars

Keeps for about 4 weeks in the fridge

1 Grate the lemons finely, taking only the very top layer of zest. Squeeze out the juice — you should have around 150 ml (5 fl oz), but a little more or less is fine.

2 Put the lemon juice, zest, sugar and butter in a heatproof bowl and place it over a saucepan of gently simmering water. Stir until the butter is melted, the sugar dissolved and all is well combined.

3 In a separate bowl, beat the eggs. Pour slowly into the lemon mixture, then whisk very frequently until the curd thickens enough to coat the back of a metal spoon (this takes about 10 minutes). The curd will thicken more as it cools and as over-cooking is the danger here, err on the side of caution.

4 Pot into warm sterilized jars (page 18), leave to cool then store in the fridge.

TIP

Have a sink of cold water at the ready, just in case. At the slightest sign that your curd is turning into scrambled eggs (the warning signs are a little white lump or two appearing in the mixture), take the bowl off the heat and stand it in the cold water, whisking frantically. You should be able to rescue it, although you may have to strain before potting.

Orange curd

A great filling for tarts and cakes, or just spread on toast, this is a little mellower than lemon curd and requires a touch less sugar. There will be tiny flecks of orange zest and the flavour is tangy, yet creamy. For a sharper taste, make when Seville oranges are in season: use the juice of one Seville and one sweet orange, and the zest of two sweet oranges.

3 oranges, preferably unwaxed

1 lemon

225 g (8 oz) granulated sugar

125 g (4½ oz) unsalted butter, cut into cubes

3 medium eggs

Makes about 3 x 227 g (8 oz) jars

Keeps for about 4 weeks in the fridge

1 Scrub the oranges well in warm water and dry them. Grate the zest from the oranges, then squeeze 2 of them and the lemon. You need around 150 ml (5 fl oz) juice.

2 Put the orange and lemon juice, orange zest, sugar and butter in a heatproof bowl over a saucepan of gently simmering water. Stir until everything is melted and dissolved.

3 In a separate bowl, beat the eggs. Add to the fruit mixture, whisking frequently until the curd thickens enough to coat the back of a metal spoon. This will take about 10 minutes. If you spot signs of curdling, follow the advice opposite. Pot into warm sterilized jars (page 18).

Lemon meringue tarts

Lemon meringue pie is a much-loved classic, and these mini versions are lovely little things. Easy to make, they are an impressive teatime treat, a light dessert or a good thing to serve at a party. They work just as well with orange curd too. And they don't stick around for long, I find...

1 Preheat the oven to 200°C (400°F). Roll out the pastry on a lightly floured surface and cut out rounds to fill mini muffin or bun tins. If you are using normal shortcrust pastry rather than the dessert variety, dust with icing sugar instead of flour when rolling out to make it slightly sweeter. Prick the cases with a fork and bake blind for 10 minutes.

2 Leave the pastry cases to cool, then fill each with lemon curd. Do not overfill or they will bubble over.

3 Whisk the egg whites until stiff, then gradually whisk in the sugar until thick and glossy.

4 Top each tart with a spoonful of meringue, lifting it into a peak with the back of a spoon. Return to the oven for about 10 minutes until the meringue is lightly browned. Leave to cool in the tins for at least 10 minutes, then ease them out and leave to cool completely on a wire rack.

375 g (13 oz) packet of ready-made shortcrust pastry (dessert pastry if possible)

175 g (6 oz) lemon curd (page 88)

2 medium egg whites

100 g (3½ oz) caster sugar

Makes about 20 tarts

Karin's lemon curd cake

I first met Karin when our young lads were newborn babes. We still meet regularly and, if I'm in luck, there may be a piece of this wonderful cake on offer. It looks fantastic and tastes even better. The recipe includes instructions for a small batch of lemon curd, but if you have a supply you can skip this part.

For the cake

225 g (8 oz) self-raising flour

1 tsp baking powder

4 medium eggs

225 g (8 oz) unsalted butter, cubed (at room temperature)

225 g (8 oz) caster sugar

1 lemon, zest and juice

For the curd

2 medium eggs

85 g (3 oz) caster sugar

1 lemon, zest and juice

50 g (1¾ oz) unsalted butter, cubed

For the icing

1 lemon, zest and juice

140 g (5 oz) icing sugar

Serves 8

1 Preheat the oven to 180 °C (350 °F). Grease and line three 20 cm (8 in) round, shallow cake tins.

2 Make the cake: sift the flour and baking powder into a large bowl and beat in the eggs, one at a time, with the butter and sugar. Beat together until smooth, but do not overbeat. Stir in the lemon zest and juice.

3 Divide the cake mixture evenly between the three cake tins and bake for 20 minutes or until firm.

4 While the cakes are cooling, make the lemon curd. Beat the eggs in a heatproof bowl. Add the sugar, lemon zest and juice, then add the butter and stir.

5 Place the bowl over a saucepan of simmering water. Whisk continuously for about 15 minutes until the mixture thickens enough to coat the back of a metal spoon. Leave to cool.

6 When cool, spread half of the lemon curd on the bottom cake. Place the middle cake on top and spread with the remaining lemon curd, and place the third cake on top.

7 Make the icing: zest the lemon and set aside. Sift the icing sugar into a bowl and add half of the lemon juice. Stir until smooth and spread over the top of a cake. Decorate with the zest.

Tropical

Mangoes and bananas

Chutney

Chutneys are simply fabulous with cheese. Or, for that matter, with pâté, with cold meats and curries, in sandwiches, with pies, savoury tarts… I rarely go a day without. But don't confine them to the side of the cheeseboard. Forget the supermarket's bewildering array of cooking sauces – 'stir-in' this, 'just-add-chicken' that. With a few chutneys in the cupboard, you have a store of delicious homemade cooking sauces to play with. Chutneys are great in stews – how about a fruity beef casserole, cooked slowly with some prunes and half a jar of autumn chutney (page 153)? Swirl some apple chutney (page 62) into crème fraîche to top a pork steak; a basic tomato sauce can be lifted a notch by a spoonful of tomato chutney (page 109); and as for sausages – they cry out to be cooked in caramelized onion marmalade (page 110).

Chutneys can be made from all manner and combinations of fruit and vegetables, cooked slowly with vinegar, sugar and spices until much of the liquid has evaporated. There's usually a fair bit of peeling and chopping involved, so they can be quite time-consuming to make and you cannot leave them unattended for too long, as they have a tendency to stick as they thicken. But even that can have its upside: 'Sorry, can't help with (*insert unpleasant task of your choice*)… I'm stirring the chutney'. Chutneys are less fussy about timings than jams and jellies – there is no setting point to worry about, and a couple of minutes more or less will not make a great deal of difference. If necessary, you can take a break in the cooking process. More than once have I realized, late at night, that I will fall asleep long before the chutney is ready to be bottled. No matter – I just turn off the heat and resume next day.

It is not unusual for chutneys to keep for several years, though they are at their best during the first year of life. Most chutneys should ideally be left to mellow and mature for a couple of months before eating – they will taste less vinegary if you can wait a while – but I confess, mine have barely cooled in the jars before I start digging in.

Mango and ginger chutney

This recipe is one of my favourites. The preparation takes a while, but it makes a large quantity and is simple to cook. Use whatever dried fruit you have in store – I like to use a mixture of raisins and apricots. This is an obvious chutney to serve with curries, but I have a great weakness for mango chutney and Cheddar cheese…

6 medium mangoes (about 2 kg (4 lb 8 oz) unprepared weight)

2 medium onions, chopped

350 g (12 oz) dried fruit

75 g (2½ oz) fresh root ginger, chopped

4 garlic cloves, crushed

2 red finger chillies, finely chopped

1 tsp ground ginger

zest and juice of 1 lime

375 ml (13 fl oz) distilled malt vinegar (or white wine vinegar)

1.2 kg (2 lb 12 oz) granulated sugar

1 tsp salt

Makes 7–8 x 340 g (12 oz) jars

Keeps for 12 months

1 Peel the mangoes and chop the flesh roughly.

2 Put all the ingredients in a preserving pan and give them a good stir. Bring slowly to the boil, stirring now and then. Cover and simmer for 15 minutes.

3 Uncover and continue to simmer, stirring from time to time, until the chutney has thickened – this should take 40–45 minutes. This chutney should have some liquid left in it, so don't cook until everything has evaporated. Pot into hot sterilized jars (page 18).

Spicy banana chutney

It was our family tradition to serve curries with sliced bananas to cool the palate and add a little sweetness. Bananas do have a particular affinity with curry and this fruity chutney really captures their flavour. It's great with poppadums and cold roast meats too.

seeds from 12 cardamom pods

500 ml (18 fl oz) distilled malt or white wine vinegar

1 tsp ground allspice

1 tsp turmeric

½ tsp cayenne pepper

450 g (1 lb) onions, chopped

1 large cooking apple, peeled, cored and chopped

75 g (2½ oz) stem ginger

60 g (2¼ oz) fresh root ginger, chopped or grated

115 g (4 oz) chopped dates

115 g (4 oz) raisins

225 g (8 oz) soft light brown sugar

½ tsp salt

6 large ripe bananas

Makes 5–6 x 340 g (12 oz) jars

Keeps for 12 months

1 Toast the cardamom seeds in a dry frying pan and grind them in a pestle and mortar. Warm 300 ml (10 fl oz) of the vinegar in a preserving pan and add all the spices.

2 While the vinegar is infusing, chop the onions and add them to the spiced vinegar. Cook for 5 minutes, then add the apple, stem ginger and fresh root ginger and simmer gently for about 15 minutes more until soft.

3 Add the remaining vinegar, dates, raisins, sugar and salt. Slice the bananas thickly into the pan. Simmer for 15–20 minutes, stirring frequently, until the chutney is thick, then pot into hot sterilized jars (page 18).

VARIATION

For a milder version, leave out the cayenne pepper and reduce the amount of fresh root ginger.

Banana jam

Bananas make an unusual jam, and this one is flavoured with all those things that bananas love: cinnamon, vanilla and rum. It is delicious on waffles and pancakes or as a sandwich filling – try it with cream cheese or peanut butter.

juice of 3 limes

juice of 1 orange, topped up with water to 175 ml (6 fl oz)

1 tsp ground cinnamon

500 g (1 lb 2 oz) granulated sugar

seeds of 1 vanilla pod (or 1 tsp vanilla bean paste)

a pinch of salt

6 large ripe bananas, sliced fairly thin or mashed

50 ml (2 fl oz) dark rum

Makes 4 x 340 g (12 oz) jars

Keeps for 3–6 months

1 Put the lime juice, orange juice and water, cinnamon, sugar, vanilla and salt in a preserving pan over a moderate heat. Stir until the sugar is completely dissolved.

2 Add the bananas and cook gently for 15–20 minutes until thick, stirring often. (Be careful as this jam has a tendency to catch.)

3 Add the rum and cook for a few minutes more, then bottle in hot sterilized jars (page 18).

VARIATION

For a banana-chocolate jam, swirl in 100 g (3½ oz) chopped or grated dark chocolate when the jam has been cooked.

Banana ice cream

I've always loved ice cream, but after a few months in America I was addicted. Back home in England, I struggled with the price of the good stuff versus the quality of the bad, so I had a go at making my own. This is my favourite to make at home. Puréeing the bananas gives a dense, creamy texture.

3 large or 4 medium bananas

juice of half a lemon

200 g (7 oz) golden caster sugar

500 ml (18 fl oz) whipping cream

Makes about 1 litre (2 pints)

1 Peel the bananas and chop roughly. Whizz in a blender or food processor with the lemon juice and sugar.

2 Add the cream and continue to blend until well mixed, then pour into an ice-cream maker. Churn accordingly, then pour into a container. If you don't have an ice-cream maker, just pour the mixture into a container and freeze for about 2 hours until ice crystals have formed around the edge, then whisk these into the middle using a fork or electric hand mixer. Return to the freezer for a couple more hours, then whisk again. Repeat if necessary, though if you can't be bothered to whisk every couple of hours, it still works – it just won't be as smooth.

VARIATIONS

Chocolate crunch ice cream

For a chocolatey version, add broken-up pieces of your favourite chocolate bar to the ice cream once it has finished churning, or stir into the freezer container when the mixture is half frozen. Try crunchy bars or balls, or broken-up chocolate biscuits.

Banana berry ripple ice cream

For a fruity ripple version, whizz 250 g (9 oz) red fruits (strawberries, raspberries, mixed berries) and 50–75 g (1¾–2½ oz) extra caster sugar in a food processor then swirl the purée into the ice cream before it is completely frozen.

Mango chicken

This recipe comes from my best friend Bernadette, who first made it for me when we were schoolchildren. It's also a great dish for a buffet, made with chicken drumsticks. Use a larger quantity of chicken so the chutney ends up as a sticky glaze rather than a sauce.

8 chicken thighs (skin on)

1 jar mango chutney, about 340 g (12 oz)

50 g (1¾ oz) fresh root ginger, grated

3 tsps ground cumin

½ tsp ground ginger

25 g (1 oz) butter

Serves 4

1 Preheat the oven to 190°C (375°F). Place the chicken thighs in an ovenproof dish and spoon the mango chutney over them. Sprinkle the ginger and ground spices on top and dot with butter.

2 Cook for 1 hour. After about 30 minutes, check to see if it is getting too brown and cover with foil if necessary.

This dish is delicious served with rice or couscous.

A really good sandwich

My taste for cheese with mango chutney started in college days. Many an essay crisis was eased by one of these from our local sandwich bar. I can never quite recreate the perfection of those – perhaps the work deadlines added a bit of extra sauce – but it's along these lines. Be generous with the filling.

1 large pitta bread

iceberg lettuce, shredded

cold roast chicken

mango chutney

Cheddar cheese, grated

mayonnaise (full-fat tastes best)

tomato and cucumber slices

freshly ground black pepper

Per person

1 Lightly toast the pitta bread, cut off one of the long edges and open.

2 Put some shredded lettuce in the bottom, then the roast chicken. Spoon mango chutney over the chicken then add a generous sprinkling of grated cheese, which will stick pleasingly to the chutney. Dollop plenty of mayonnaise on top, then finish with alternate slices of tomato and cucumber and a good grinding of black pepper.

Eat in the sunshine.

Now get back to work.

A simple curry

This basic recipe can be adapted to your taste; if you like it fiery add more dried chillies. It works well with other meats too. Serve with basmati rice, naan bread, some natural yoghurt and lots of chutney – mango and ginger chutney (page 96) or spicy banana chutney (page 97) go perfectly.

3 tbsp sunflower or vegetable oil

1 large onion, chopped

3 whole cardamom pods

a pinch of dried chillies,
or more according to taste

3 garlic cloves, crushed

1 tsp ground ginger

1 tsp ground coriander

1 tsp ground cumin

1 tsp turmeric

2 tsp tomato purée

500 ml (18 fl oz) hot water

600 g (1 lb 5 oz) chicken breasts or thigh (boneless, skinless), cut into bite-sized pieces

1 tbsp natural yoghurt

1 heaped tsp cornflour

a large pinch of salt

Serves 4

1 Heat the oil in a heavy-based saucepan and cook the onions for 3–4 minutes over a medium heat, stirring occasionally. Add the cardamoms and dried chilli and cook for a further 3–4 minutes. Turn down the heat and stir in the garlic. Cook over a low heat for 15 minutes, stirring now and then.

2 Add the ground spices and cook for 2 minutes, then stir in the tomato purée. Pour in the hot water and give it all a good stir.

3 Add the chicken pieces and simmer for 20 minutes over a moderate heat.

4 Put the yoghurt, cornflour and salt in a small bowl and beat together well. Stir into the curry and simmer for 3–4 minutes more, until the sauce has thickened.

VARIATIONS

Prawn or chickpea curry

Follow steps 1 and 2. Simmer the sauce for about 15 minutes, then add a 400 g (14 oz) tin of drained, cooked chickpeas or 450 g (1 lb) cooked king prawns.

For a more substantial curry, add some vegetables – cubed aubergine, thickly sliced courgettes, cauliflower florets and okra are good. Add them 5–10 minutes before the end, depending on the cooking times of the vegetables you use.

Wholesome

Tomatoes, onions and courgettes

Sauces and ketchups

Ketchup has its origins in China and Malaysia, and the first ketchups produced by Westerners back in the 1700s were probably made from mushrooms or walnuts. The tomato variety so popular today took another hundred years to come along. One of the earliest recipes for tomato ketchup appears in an American cookbook of 1801. It requires you to take 100 ripe tomatoes and squeeze them to a pulp with your bare hands, before boiling them for two hours with salt and pushing through a sieve with a silver spoon. The purée is then mixed with spices (mace, nutmeg, allspice, cloves, cinnamon, ginger and pepper), and simmered until thick. Two hundred years later the basics are little changed, though we now add vinegar and sugar, both to give a sweet-and-sour taste and to act as a preservative. Part of me thinks that squishing the tomatoes with your hands would be a lot of fun – cleaning up afterwards rather less so.

Ketchups and sauces are a great way of using up a glut of very ripe fruit and vegetables. The method is this: cook your chosen produce to a pulp, then pass through a sieve or a mouli, add vinegar and sugar and simmer until much of the liquid has evaporated and the sauce has thickened. Season with a selection of spices.

Use the sauces and ketchups as they are to dunk your chips, sausages, oriental snacks and much more. They have their place in cooking too: brush onto meat; add to marinades; create a dip by thinning them with a little soy sauce or vinegar; stir into stews and sauces…and keep in the back of your mind that image of the 19th-century cook, merrily squashing ripe tomatoes on a summer's day.

Tomato ketchup

Summer is in full swing and ripe tomatoes are piled high and cheap – now is the time to make ketchup. The homemade variety has more texture and spice and, well, a little more class than shop-bought. Chips and ketchup are inseparable, and no barbecue should be without it. In cooking, use to add depth to tomato sauces – for pasta, meatballs or homemade baked beans.

1.2 kg (2 lb 12 oz) ripe tomatoes, roughly chopped

1 large onion, chopped

1 red pepper, deseeded and chopped

1 cooking apple, cored and roughly chopped (no need to peel)

2 garlic cloves, chopped

300 ml (10 fl oz) red wine vinegar

150 g (5½ oz) soft light brown or light muscovado sugar

a large pinch of sea salt

½ tsp ground allspice

¼ tsp ground cloves

¼ tsp ground cinnamon

¼ tsp ground coriander

freshly ground black pepper

Makes 1 litre (2 pints)

Keeps for 6–9 months

1 Put the tomatoes, onion, red pepper, apple and garlic in a preserving pan. Cook over a gentle heat, stirring often at the beginning, for about 30 minutes until soft and pulpy.

2 Allow to cool slightly then push through a sieve or a mouli. Wash the preserving pan and put the purée back in, together with the vinegar, sugar, salt and spices. Heat gently, stirring until the sugar has dissolved.

3 Simmer for 20–30 minutes until thickened (it will thicken more on cooling), then pour into hot sterilized bottles or jars (page 18).

VARIATIONS

For a spicier ketchup, add some fresh or dried chillies to the mix in step 1.

Experiment with spices: try celery seed, mace or a bay leaf.

Replace some of the light sugar with a little dark muscovado for a deeper flavour.

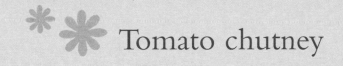

Tomato chutney

This is another favourite from my mother's recipe collection. I think of this as ketchup for grown-ups – it goes well with the same foods and, like tomato ketchup, a little of this chutney perks up a tomato sauce.

1.8 kg (4 lb) ripe tomatoes

225 g (8 oz) shallots or pickling onions, chopped

4 tsp salt

4 tbsp mustard seeds

1 tbsp allspice berries

6 peppercorns

225 g (8 oz) granulated sugar

425 ml (15 fl oz) distilled malt vinegar

Makes about 4 x 340 g (12 oz) jars

Keeps for 12 months

1 Cut a cross in the base of each tomato, then place them in a large bowl. Pour boiling water over, leave for a minute or two, then remove the skins. Chop roughly and place in a large pan with the onions and salt.

2 Tie the spices in a piece of muslin and add to the pan. Cook over a low heat, stirring, for about 30 minutes until the tomatoes are reduced to a pulp.

3 Add the sugar and vinegar and stir until the sugar has dissolved. Bring to the boil then lower the heat and simmer for 20–25 minutes, stirring occasionally, until the chutney thickens.

4 Remove the spice bag and pot into hot sterilized jars (page 18).

Caramelized onion marmalade

Despite its name, this is not one for your breakfast toast*, but a fabulous accompaniment to sausages, burgers and strong cheeses. Use it as a cooking ingredient too – a spoonful or two in gravy or casseroles adds a real depth of flavour. Use white sugar or a mixture of white and muscovado sugars for a darker, more treacly result.

4 tbsp olive oil

2 kg (4 lb 8 oz) red or white onions, thinly sliced

300 g (10½ oz) sugar (white granulated, muscovado or a mixture)

300 ml (10 fl oz) red wine vinegar

250 ml (9 fl oz) red wine

3 tbsp balsamic vinegar

3 garlic cloves, crushed

2 tsp wholegrain mustard

a pinch of paprika

a pinch of dried chillies

1 bay leaf

salt and pepper

Makes about 6–7 x 340 g (12 oz) jars

Keeps for 6–9 months

1 Heat the oil in a large heavy-based pan and fry the onions for 10 minutes over a moderate heat.

2 Add 100 g (3½ oz) of the sugar and cook for a further 10 minutes, stirring occasionally, until soft. Make sure it does not burn.

3 Add all the remaining ingredients to the pan and simmer for 25–30 minutes until most of the liquid has evaporated, then pot into hot sterilized jars (page 18).

TIP

All that onion-chopping makes your hands smell. To remove the whiff, rub a few drops of lemon juice onto your hands (or rub the inside of a used lemon shell over your hands).

* Unless you are as onion-mad as my son James: 'What would you rather have, a piece of chocolate or a piece of onion?'

James: 'How big's the onion?'

Growing your own

Homemade jams and chutneys are infinitely tastier than most shop-bought varieties. The same goes for homegrown produce too, but that doesn't mean you have to spend your life gardening. The pleasures of growing your own can be enjoyed by anyone, even if you have the tiniest patch and limited time. A separate vegetable plot is by no means essential – just use whatever space you have. The pots on my patio filled with geraniums in the summer occasionally house a tomato plant or two instead. A bare patch where a sandpit once stood is home to a courgette plant; and the blackcurrant bush, bought on impulse and currently awaiting a home, will have to rub shoulders with a peony. I have even been known to stick a couple of cabbages amongst the flowers. Why not? Even if you have no outside space, a sunny windowsill is all you need to grow pots of herbs. A few leaves can transform a dish, and larger quantities can be made into pesto or dried for teas.

My rather haphazard approach may not receive the approval of those with greener fingers than mine – if I'm honest, I enjoy the picking (and of course the pickling) more than the planting. Never mind. I stick to the things that work for me, those crops for which I have both the time and the space: tomatoes, courgettes and runner beans have flourished without too much hand-holding, and there are herbs aplenty.

So have a look around your house, your balcony, your garden and find a spot to plant something edible: grow mustard and cress on damp tissue paper on the kitchen windowsill, plant a pot of herbs, get a blueberry bush for a tub, set a single runner bean plant on an upward course for the giant's castle…And enjoy eating the results.

Courgette fritters

I once enjoyed a memorable lunch in a shady courtyard in the Greek city of Thessaloniki. Many good things were on the menu, but golden courgette fritters made the biggest impression. This is my attempt to recreate them. Eat hot with pitta bread, a garlicky yoghurt dip and some lemon wedges.

4 medium courgettes

250 ml (9 fl oz) beer or lager (non-alcoholic varieties work just as well)

150 g (5½ oz) plain flour

1 tbsp tomato ketchup

a generous pinch of salt

sunflower oil or mild olive oil for frying

For the yoghurt dip

350 g (12 oz) Greek yoghurt (or thick, natural yoghurt)

1 fat garlic clove, crushed

black pepper

a pinch of paprika

Serves 6 as a light lunch

1 Wash the courgettes and trim the ends. Slice lengthways very thinly.

2 Make the batter: pour the beer into a bowl and whisk in the flour, ketchup and salt.

3 Heat about 5 mm (¼ in) of the oil in a heavy frying pan. Dip the courgette slices in the batter, shake off any excess and fry until cooked and golden-brown. Turn them once – they take about 2 minutes on each side. (You may need to top up the oil from time to time.) Drain on kitchen paper and keep warm while you fry the rest.

4 Make the dip: stir the yogurt and garlic together and season with a grinding of black pepper and a pinch of paprika.

Tante Betty's courgette pickles

My great aunts Tante Trude and Tante Betty, lived a few streets from each other in Innsbruck, Austria and my brother and I spent many a happy summer there. At Tante Trude's house we ate clear soup and goulash, perhaps with my favourite *Serviettenknödel*, a loaf-shaped steamed dumpling. Tante Betty was a little less traditional; her pizzas were legendary and she was particularly proud of her homegrown courgettes, which she made into these delicious pickles.

900 g (2 lb) courgettes,
thinly sliced

225 g (8 oz) onions, thinly sliced

850 ml (1½ pts) water

100 g (3½ oz) salt

425 g (15 oz) sugar

450 ml (16 fl oz) cider vinegar

1 tsp celery seeds

1 tsp ground turmeric

½ tsp prepared mustard

2 tsp yellow mustard seeds

Makes 4–5 x 340 g (12 oz) jars

Store in the fridge, where they will keep for at least 3 months

1 Place the vegetables in a large heatproof bowl. Cover with the water and stir in the salt. Leave to stand for 2 hours, then drain well and pat dry with kitchen paper. Return to the bowl.

2 Put the sugar, vinegar and spices into a saucepan and heat to boiling point. Pour the liquid over the vegetables and leave to stand for 2 hours.

3 Transfer the whole lot to a preserving pan and bring to the boil. Boil for 5 minutes, stirring occasionally, then pack into hot sterilized jars (page 18), making sure that the vegetables are covered with the pickling liquid.

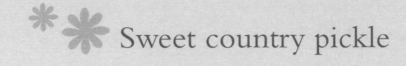

Sweet country pickle

Dark and spicy, this sweet pickle comes into its own when eaten with some good strong cheese and crusty bread, alongside a pork pie or with generous slices of carved ham. It takes a while to prepare all the vegetables so make a cup of tea, put the radio on and get chopping.

4 medium carrots, diced

1 small swede, diced

1 medium cauliflower, cut up into smallish pieces (a similar size to the other veg)

1 large onion, chopped

1 large courgette, diced

2 crisp eating apples
(eg Granny Smith), diced

125 g (4½ oz) dates, chopped
(or a mixture of dates and raisins)

100 g (3½ oz) gherkins, chopped

225 g (8 oz) dark muscovado sugar

600 ml (1 pint) distilled malt vinegar

juice of 1 lemon

1 tsp dark soy sauce

1 tsp mustard seeds

2 tsp ground allspice

a pinch of dried chilli flakes

**Makes about 6 x 340 g
(12 oz) jars**

Keeps for 6–9 months

1 Once you have completed the marathon chop, put all the ingredients in a preserving pan and stir well to combine them.

2 Bring to the boil, then reduce the heat and simmer for about 1–1¼ hours until most of the liquid has evaporated and the vegetables are cooked but still retain a little bite. Stir occasionally and more frequently towards the end of cooking.

3 Pot into hot sterilized jars (page 18). Leave to mature for a couple of weeks before eating.

Tomato and courgette chutney

Tomatoes, courgettes and onions are a fantastic trio and make a colourful chutney. Courgettes are easy to grow. Baby ones are delicious raw or gently cooked – leave them to grow and you will end up with far bigger courgettes to stuff and bake. If using very large ones here, you may need to peel and deseed them first.

800 g (1 lb 12 oz) tomatoes, roughly chopped

800 g (1 lb 12 oz) green or yellow courgettes, cut into small cubes

500 g (1 lb 2 oz) onions, chopped

700 g (1 lb 9 oz) granulated sugar

600 ml (1 pint) cider vinegar or white wine vinegar

2 cm (¾ in) piece of fresh root ginger, finely chopped

1 tsp ground coriander

a pinch of dried chilli flakes

1 tsp salt

black pepper

Makes about 6 x 340 g (12 oz) jars

Keeps for 12 months

1 Put all the ingredients into a preserving pan and heat gently, stirring, until the sugar has dissolved.

2 Bring the mixture to the boil, then reduce the heat and simmer for about 1¼ hours until the chutney is well reduced. The thicker it gets, the more often you need to stir – towards the end you need to give it your full stirring attention to ensure that it doesn't burn.

3 Pot the chutney into hot sterilized jars (page 18). If you can, leave it for a couple of weeks to mature.

117

Aromatic

Herbs and spices

Jellies

In late summer, when the Bramleys are ripening, endless windfalls are there for the taking. A happy ending awaits those imperfect apples lying on the ground: destined for the preserving pan, they will provide the base of all manner of jellies. In order to set well, jellies must be made with pectin-rich fruit otherwise you will end up with syrup. You can add pectin, but using tart apples in the recipe gives great results.

I am rather new to this kind of preserve-making and last year I experimented with numerous flavours – lavender and lemon, red pepper, pink grapefruit with pomegranate seeds, a deep-coloured bramble jelly and an intense hedgerow jelly made with elderberries (page 154). Bear in mind that a large pile of fruit will end up as a few pots of jelly, so if you only have a limited amount of your favourite fruit, making jelly is probably not the best thing to do with it.

One of the delights of jelly making is that preparation of the fruit can be as haphazard as you like – there is no need to peel or chop neatly. It's a two-stage process: first, the fruit is cooked until soft and then left to drip through a jelly bag or large sieve lined with a clean tea towel. Next hang up the 'Do Not Disturb' sign and forget about it for a day or night. When it has dripped until it can drip no more, measure the liquid, add the requisite amount of sugar and boil until it sets. A good jelly should be wobbly, clear and shining with jewel-like colours. Paler jellies lend themselves well to the addition of flecks of herbs, spices or fruit seeds, attractively suspended in the jars.

Jellies are delicious with practically anything. The herb jellies (on page 123) are excellent with meats, but equally at home on a cheese board. Fill a sponge cake with thick cream and bramble jelly (page 154). The strong-flavoured hedgerow jelly can hold its own with game dishes and goes surprisingly well with the Potato, pear and blue cheese gratin (page 70). Heat them and they melt, which makes them useful as glazes or for adding flavour to soups, stews and gravies.

Herb jellies

Chopped herbs look pretty suspended in an apple-based jelly. Sage, mint, rosemary, thyme or tarragon are all excellent options, or use a mixture. Herb jellies go well with hot or cold roast meats – sage with pork, tarragon with chicken, and mint or rosemary with lamb.

1.5 kg (3 lb 5 oz) cooking apples (windfalls are fine), roughly chopped

1 litre (1¾ pints) water

1 lemon, juice and shells

8 sprigs fresh herbs

500 g (1 lb 2 oz) white granulated sugar per 600 ml (1 pint) juice

Makes about 4 x 340 g (12 oz) jars

Keeps for 6–9 months

1 Chop the apples roughly, cutting out any bad bits and removing the stalks. (No need to peel or core.)

2 Put the apples, water, lemon juice and shells in a preserving pan with 6 of the herb sprigs. Bring to the boil and simmer for 30–40 minutes until the apples are completely soft.

3 Pour the apple mixture into a scalded jelly bag (page 12) and leave it to drip for 6–8 hours, or overnight, into a large clean bowl or jug. It is tempting to squeeze the bag – don't. It will make the jelly cloudy and we're after a clear jelly here.

4 Measure the juice and pour into the cleaned preserving pan. For each 600 ml (1 pint) of juice, add 500 g (1 lb 2 oz) sugar. Heat gently and stir until the sugar has dissolved. Bring to the boil and boil rapidly for 5–10 minutes, then test for a set (page 18).

5 Leave the jelly to cool for 10 minutes. Meanwhile, strip the leaves from the remaining 2 herb sprigs and chop finely. Stir the chopped herbs gently into the jelly, then pot into hot sterilized jars (page 18). Tip the jars as they cool to distribute the herbs.

Pesto

A vibrant combination of pounded basil leaves, garlic, hard cheese such as Parmesan or Pecorino, pine nuts and olive oil, pesto has been flavouring the pasta dishes of northern Italy for centuries. The pesto you buy in jars, whizzed to within an inch of its life, is a far cry from the real thing. The first time I ate fresh pesto was a revelation – vibrant, coarse-textured, deeply aromatic. Making it for the first time was no less of a discovery when I realized just how simple it is. Once you have tried the two recipes on pages 126 and 127, use them as a springboard for creating your own – vary the nuts, the herbs, the cheese, even the oil. Purists might mutter, but there are myriad combinations out there with which to experiment. And don't confine them to a bowl of pasta. Here are a few ideas for pesto recipes and uses to get you started:

• Rosemary and walnut pesto (rub into a leg of lamb before roasting)

• Sage and almond pesto (stir into wide ribbons of buttered pasta)

• Parsley pesto (with boiled new potatoes or a potato salad)

• Tarragon pesto (mix with breadcrumbs as a crust for chicken or fish)

• Sun-dried tomato and black olive pesto (spread on toasted rustic bread and top with fresh sliced tomatoes for instant bruschetta)

• Add a spoonful of pesto to salad dressings

• Thin pesto with a little olive oil and drizzle over a thick soup, topped with croutons

• Dot small spoonfuls of pesto onto a pizza (excellent on toppings such as goats'cheese, chicken or chargrilled peppers)

• Stir a little basil pesto into freshly cooked pasta then top with toasted pine nuts, torn basil leaves and grated Parmesan

• Stir the pesto of your choice into mashed potatoes

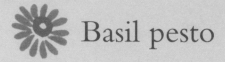

Basil pesto

Pounding the ingredients in a pestle and mortar is the traditional way to make pesto, but I usually go for the easier option of a food processor. This recipe is based on instructions given to me by an Italian friend and the measuring is done with your hands rather than kitchen scales.

2 handfuls of pine nuts

2 handfuls of basil leaves (no stalks)

a pinch of salt

2–3 garlic cloves, peeled

3 tbsp extra-virgin olive oil, plus a little more for the jar

2 handfuls of grated Parmesan or Grana Padano cheese

a squeeze of lemon juice (optional)

freshly ground black pepper

Makes 1 227 g (8 oz) jar (enough for 6 people to stir into their pasta)

Keeps in the fridge for about 2 weeks or the freezer for 6 months

1 Toast the pine nuts in a hot, dry frying pan for about 2 minutes (shake the pan every 30 seconds) until lightly browned.

2 Put the basil, pine nuts, salt, garlic and olive oil in a food processor and whizz until chopped but do not over-process – it should still retain some texture.

3 Add the cheese and pulse for a few seconds. Taste it – add a squeeze of lemon juice and some black pepper if you wish. If the consistency is too thick, add more olive oil.

4 Spoon the pesto into a clean jar and pour a layer of oil on top.

Rocket and walnut pesto

Peppery rocket makes a good alternative to classic basil pesto. This recipe is quite heavy on the garlic so if you are not a huge fan you may want to adjust the amount accordingly. Stir into pasta for an instant supper dish – spaghetti or linguine are good – or try the bread below.

100 g (3½ oz) walnuts

100 g (3½ oz) rocket

juice of ½ lemon

a big pinch of salt

3 garlic cloves, peeled

150 ml (5 fl oz) olive oil

100 g (3½ oz) finely grated Parmesan or Pecorino cheese

freshly ground black pepper

Makes enough to fill one 454 g (1 lb) jar

Keeps in the fridge for about 2 weeks or in the freezer for 6 months

1 Toast the walnuts for a couple of minutes in a hot, dry frying pan to bring out their flavour (a cast iron pan is perfect if you have one).

2 Put the rocket, walnuts, lemon juice, salt, garlic and a little of the olive oil in a food processor and whizz until roughly chopped, but don't overdo it. Add the rest of the olive oil and pulse for a few seconds to combine.

3 Stir in the cheese and season with a good grinding of black pepper. If you want a thinner consistency, add extra olive oil.

4 Spoon into a clean jar and pour a layer of oil on top.

Rocket and walnut pesto bread

Thanks to our neighbour Daniel for this idea.

Take one crusty loaf of bread (baguette, ciabatta or medium-sized white loaf) and a good helping of rocket and walnut pesto. Make deep diagonal slits in the loaf at 2 cm (¾ in) intervals. Slather pesto into the slits. Wrap in foil and bake in a preheated oven 200°C (400°F) for about 15 minutes.

Flavoured oils

Capture the flavour and aroma of herbs and spices in a bottle. If you want the oil as a background, use a mild olive or sunflower oil; stronger oils such as extra-virgin olive oil will add their own flavour to the mix. Flavoured oils have many uses: in dressings, to marinade meat, to drizzle over pizzas and pasta, as a dip for bread, or simply use them for cooking in place of plain oil.

Oil is not a long-term preserving method in a domestic kitchen. Make sure that all ingredients and bottles are scrupulously clean and dry. Keep the oils refrigerated and use in the recommended time.

Herb oil

250 ml (9 fl oz) mild olive oil

1 small sprig of sage

1 small sprig of thyme

1 small sprig of rosemary

1 bay leaf

5 black peppercorns

Makes 1 x 250 ml (9 fl oz) bottle

Keeps in the fridge for 2–3 weeks

1 Wash the herbs and pat them completely dry, then spread on a clean cloth and leave to dry further for 24 hours in a warm place.

2 Put the herbs and peppercorns in a clean, dry, sterilized glass bottle. Pour the olive oil over the herbs, making sure they are completely covered. Seal tightly and store in the fridge.

TIP

For the best results, pick herbs on a warm dry day.

Chilli oil

450 ml (16 fl oz) mild olive oil

15 g (½ oz) dried chilli flakes

10 whole dried chillies

Makes 1 x 450 ml (16 fl oz) bottle

Keeps for several months

1 Push the whole dried chillies into a clean, sterilized glass bottle and tip in the chilli flakes – a funnel is useful for this.

2 Pour the oil into the bottle, close tightly and shake it well. Store the oil somewhere cool and dark and leave to infuse for a week or two. Give it a shake every day if you remember.

TIP

The oil will get stronger over time. Strain it if you do not want it to get any hotter, or top up with extra oil as you use it.

Chilli jam

This is a versatile preserve to have in your storecupboard. It tastes brilliant with sausages, barbecued meats and in sandwiches; thin it down with a little vinegar and you have a dipping sauce for oriental snacks. It's a marvellous cooking ingredient too, wonderful in stir-fries and sauces, or drizzled over toasted goats' cheese (see page 135).

For a hot chilli jam

5–6 medium red peppers
(or a mix of red and yellow)

4 hot red chillies
(eg scotch bonnet, birds' eye)

2–4 mild-medium long red chillies

zest and juice of 2 limes
(or 1 lemon and 1 lime)

350 ml (12 fl oz) red or white
wine vinegar

1.3 kg (3 lb) white granulated sugar

125–250 ml (4–9 fl oz) liquid
pectin

2 tbsp sweet paprika

**For a mild version, use 4–6 mild
red chillies**

Makes 7–8 x 227 g (8 oz) jars

Keeps for 6–9 months

1 Deseed the peppers and chillies, chop them roughly and place in a food processor with the lime zest and about half the juice. Whizz to a fine pulp – you will have a vibrant, heady-smelling purée.

2 Tip the purée into a preserving pan (this mixture bubbles up tremendously so use a large pan) and add the remaining lemon or lime juice, vinegar and sugar. Use the vinegar to swill out the food processor bowl so all the chilli juices end up in the pan. Warm the mixture gently until the sugar is dissolved. If you missed any seeds, fish them out with a teaspoon at this stage.

3 Turn up the heat and boil for 10 minutes. Keep an eye on it, though, as it bubbles up like billy-o. Remove from the heat and stir in the paprika and the pectin. If you want a fairly runny jam, use 125 ml (4 fl oz) pectin; use more if you want something firmer.

4 Return to the heat and boil for a further 3–4 minutes before testing for a set (page 18). If the jam is too runny, boil again for another 3 minutes and test again. Pot into hot sterilized jars (page 18).

TIP

I urge you to wear rubber or latex gloves when chopping the chillies (and I speak from bitter, finger-burning experience).

Wholegrain mustard

Mustard is very easy to make – there is no actual cooking involved, just soaking, mixing and blending – and it keeps for years. I like to use a fruity ale, but any beer will do. Use the mustard in a vinaigrette dressing; add a spoonful to the batter for toad-in-the-hole or to a cheese sauce; serve with sausages and cold roast beef; spread thinly on a toasted cheese sandwich...

100 g (3½ oz) yellow mustard seeds

100 g (3½ oz) black mustard seeds

200 ml (7 fl oz) beer

80 ml (3 fl oz) cider vinegar

1 tbsp balsamic vinegar

1 tsp freshly grated nutmeg

a pinch of ground ginger

a pinch of cinnamon

1 tbsp sea salt

4 tbsp runny honey

Makes approx 2 x 340 g (12 oz) jars

Keeps for several years (if it dries out, stir in a little vinegar)

1 Mix the mustard seeds in a bowl or jug and pour in the beer, vinegars and spices. Cover with a clean tea towel and leave to soak for at least 8 hours or overnight.

2 Add the salt and honey and stir well. Warm the honey jar (minus lid) in the microwave for a few seconds so it is easier to measure.

3 Whizz the mixture in a food processor to break up the mustard seeds until it is the desired consistency. This can take a good few minutes – the longer you process it, the smoother it will be. Scrape down the sides with a spatula from time to time. The mustard will be fairly runny, but it will thicken in the jar as the mustard seeds absorb the liquid.

4 Spoon or pour through a funnel into hot sterilized jars (page 18). Push the mustard down with a teaspoon to remove any air bubbles. Ideally, you should leave it for a few weeks to mature, but if your sausages can't wait, dig in.

TIP

If the mustard does not process well, strain off some of the liquid and try again. Add the strained liquid once the seeds are processed.

Thai red curry paste

Infinitely tastier and more aromatic than the shop-bought variety, this homemade paste is the foundation of a stunning curry, and can be used in stir-fries too. It is easier to process in bulk, and keeps well in the freezer, so you might as well make a big batch. It freezes into a crumbly mass, rather than a rock-solid lump, so it is easy to dig out frozen spoonfuls as required.

3 long fresh red chillies

2 long dried red chillies

4 small hot dried red chillies

2 stalks lemon grass, cut up into very small pieces (use kitchen scissors to do this)

1 tsp salt

4 garlic cloves

2.5 cm (1 in) fresh galangal, peeled and chopped (if you can't get it, use fresh root ginger instead)

3 small shallots, roughly chopped

5 lime leaves (if fresh, chop finely; if dried, crumble and remove any hard stalks)

1 tsp ground coriander

1 tsp ground cumin

2 tsp nam pla (fish sauce) or light soy sauce

1 tsp fresh lime juice

Makes about 5 tablespoons (enough for 5–6 curries, each serving 4)

1 Combine all the ingredients in a food processor and whizz until chopped – it will be a fairly rough paste and you need to scrape down the sides often.

2 Transfer the curry paste to a lidded container and freeze. That's it.

When you want to use some, break off/scoop out the required amount and cook from frozen.

TIP

I've said it before and I'll say it again: wear gloves when you chop chillies!

VARIATION

For a Thai green curry paste replace the red chillies (fresh and dried) with 4 long finger chillies plus 4 small green chillies, chopped and deseeded.

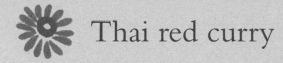

Thai red curry

Real fast food at its absolute best. Once the ingredients are prepared (and even that is not terribly time-consuming), it can be ready in minutes. Thai curries are much quicker to cook than Indian curries, and more liquid – almost like a soup. If you can't find Thai aubergines, use 150 g (5½ oz) baby sweetcorn instead. Serve with Thai fragrant rice.

1 tbsp sunflower or vegetable oil

1 tbsp red curry paste (see opposite)

400 g (14 oz) tin coconut milk

500 g (1 lb 2 oz) chicken breast, cut into bite-sized pieces

150 g (5½ oz) button mushrooms, cut into quarters

4–5 Thai aubergines, cut into wedges

1 red pepper, deseeded and cut into strips

1 tbsp nam pla (fish sauce) or light soy sauce

1 tsp sugar (palm sugar if you can get it, otherwise white or light brown sugar)

10 basil leaves (Holy basil if possible)

a handful of coriander leaves, roughly chopped, to garnish

Serves 4

1 Heat the oil in a wok. Add the curry paste and cook, stirring, for about 20 seconds.

2 Turn the heat right down and pour in the coconut milk. Stir well and warm gently, then increase the heat and bring to the boil.

3 Add the chicken and vegetables and simmer until they are cooked (about 4–5 minutes).

4 Add the nam pla (or soy sauce), sugar and basil leaves and cook for a minute more. Garnish with coriander and serve.

VARIATION

This recipe also works well made with beef. Or use king prawns, adding them a couple of minutes after the vegetables.

Toasted goats' cheese salad

with chilli jam

Here is a delicious supper for two involving minimal effort and time. If you've made the chilli jam, that's most of it done. A rustic crusty bread and a log-like goats' cheese (*bûche de chevre*) are perfect. Use some soft leaves such as lamb's lettuce, baby spinach and perhaps a little rocket. Avoid anything too peppery as goats' cheese and chilli jam are both strong flavours.

2–4 thick slices of bread (enough for 2 people)

butter, to spread on the bread

4 thick slices goats' cheese – the firm type with a rind, about 7 cm (2¾ in) diameter

2 big handfuls of salad leaves

1 tbsp olive oil

1 tbsp balsamic vinegar

1–2 tbsp chilli jam (page 130)

Serves 2 as a substantial supper (or 4 people as a starter)

1 Toast the bread on one side under a medium hot grill. Place it on a baking tray to catch any cheesy spills later on. Turn the bread over and butter the uncooked side, then top with the goats' cheese. Grill for about 4–5 minutes until the cheese is lightly browned and bubbling.

2 While the cheese is toasting, divide the salad leaves between two plates. Whisk the oil and vinegar together and pour over the salad. If the chilli jam is firm, stir in a little water or vinegar and warm in a microwave for a few seconds.

3 Place the goats' cheese toasts on top of the salad leaves and drizzle the jam over the cheese.

Tomato and mozzarella tart

This simple tart, with its topping of juicy tomatoes and melting cheese, is a little reminiscent of a pizza. It makes a perfect summer lunch tart to be eaten warm with a large green salad and a nice chilled glass of something.

375 g (13 oz) ready-made puff pastry

a little milk or beaten egg, to glaze

4–5 ripe tomatoes (about 425 g/15 oz)

250 g (9 oz) mozzarella

100 g (3½ oz) pesto (page 126)

black pepper

a few basil leaves

Serves 6

1 Preheat the oven to 200°C (400°F). Roll out the pastry into a rectangle approximately 25 x 40 cm (10 x 16 in) and place on a large baking sheet. Score a line 2 cm (¾ in) in from the edges. Brush the edges with a little milk or beaten egg and prick the inner rectangle with a fork.

2 Bake blind for 10 minutes. Slice the tomatoes and mozzarella into rounds (not too thin).

3 Remove the pastry from the oven, spread most of the pesto over the inner rectangle, then cover with the sliced tomatoes. Lay the slices of mozzarella on top of the tomatoes, then dot the remaining pesto over the tart.

4 Return the tart to the oven and bake for a further 10–15 minutes until the pastry is golden and the cheese is gooey and starting to brown. Before serving, give the tart a grinding of black pepper and scatter with basil leaves.

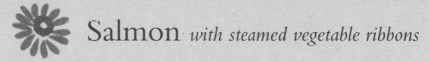

Salmon *with steamed vegetable ribbons*

Here is another quick and easy supper for two. This recipe evolved from the contents of my vegetable drawer, and I make it often. Vary the vegetables depending on what you have in stock (I often just use carrot and leek), but the ginger is essential. Serve with egg noodles or rice.

2 salmon fillets, 125 g (4½ oz) each

1 tbsp chilli jam (page 130)

1 large carrot, peeled

1 courgette

1 leek

2 cm (¾ in) fresh root ginger, chopped into matchsticks

rice or noodles, to serve

Serves 2

1 Preheat the oven to 200°C (400°C). Place each salmon fillet on a rectangle of kitchen foil and put a teaspoonful of chilli jam on top. Make loose parcels with the foil, place on a baking tray and cook in the oven for 20–25 minutes.

2 While the salmon is cooking, prepare the vegetables. Use a potato peeler to cut both into long thin ribbons. Cut the leek in half widthways, then slice lengthways into quarters. Put the prepared vegetables and ginger in a bowl and mix them together.

3 If you are cooking rice, start it 10 minutes before the salmon is due out of the oven. Put the vegetables and ginger on to steam 5 minutes before the salmon is due to be ready. If cooking rice or noodles, time it so that they will be ready at the same time as the salmon and vegetables.

4 In each bowl place some rice or noodles, then a layer of steamed vegetable ribbons. Place a salmon fillet on top of the vegetables. Drizzle with a little extra chilli jam (warm it a little if it is too thick) and a dash of soy sauce.

VARIATION

Try making this with Chinese plum sauce (page 50) instead of chilli jam.

Potato wedges

with chilli jam and sour cream

This is a great dish for lounging about with and popular with children and adults alike. Share a plateful over a beer or two, or serve as an accompaniment to something meaty. I don't fancy using a deep fat fryer, so this is the closest I get to homemade chips (and these are a lot healthier).

about 4–5 large potatoes
(such as Desiree or Maris Piper)

1 tbsp olive or sunflower oil

sea salt

½ jar chilli jam, about 115 g/4 oz
(page 130)

150 ml (5 fl oz) pot of sour cream

Serves 4

1 Preheat the oven to 220°C (425°F). Cut each potato into thick wedges (there is no need to peel).

2 Place the wedges in a single layer on a large baking or roasting tray and drizzle with the oil. Use more than one tray if necessary. Stir the wedges around to coat them and crumble some flakes of sea salt over them.

3 Roast in the oven for about 40 minutes until cooked through and golden-brown. Shake them around a bit halfway through cooking (use a fish slice to dislodge any that stick).

Eat hot, with a bowl of chilli jam and some sour cream for dipping.

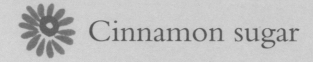

Cinnamon sugar

My mother always had a jar of cinnamon sugar to hand, and so do I – no store cupboard should be without it. Making cinnamon sugar is so basic I'm not sure that it counts as a recipe. However, having seen jars of it on sale at frankly exorbitant prices, and as many people tell me that they are not sure what to do with it, I feel bound to tell you more.

225 g (8 oz) white granulated sugar

1 tbsp ground cinnamon

You will need a clean, dry, lidded jam jar with a capacity of 300 ml (10 fl oz) for this amount.

Place the sugar and cinnamon in the jar and stir them together well with a teaspoon. Screw the lid on tightly and shake until combined.

It is not an exact science – these proportions make a well flavoured sugar. Add less cinnamon if you prefer. Use at every available opportunity – you can easily make more when you run out.

• Enjoy it on hot buttered toast, pancakes or waffles

• Sprinkle on cakes and biscuits before baking

• Stir into natural yogurt

• Add a spoonful to a fruit salad

• Sprinkle it on your porridge

• Use a little in cakes or crumbles in place of regular sugar

• Shake over banana or apple fritters

• Sweeten stewed fruit

• Dredge doughnuts in it

• Mix with raisins or sultanas to stuff baked apples

• Swirl into fruit breads

Vanilla sugar

If you have used vanilla seeds in a recipe, don't throw away the pods – they still have plenty of flavour. Even if the whole pod has been used, no problem. Simply rinse, leave to dry and it's ready to go again. A pod in a jar of sugar will impart a delicate flavour and it has numerous uses. Not only does it appeal to my taste buds, but fits pleasingly with my 'no wastage' ethos.

225 g (8 oz) white caster sugar

1 used vanilla pod, broken into 2–3 pieces, or ½ an unused vanilla pod

You will need a clean, dry, lidded jam jar with a capacity of 300 ml (10 fl oz) for this amount.

Pour the sugar into a clean, dry jam jar with a screw-top lid and bury the vanilla pod pieces in the sugar. Close tightly and give it a good shake. If you are using a new pod, split it lengthways and scrape the sticky seeds into the sugar, then stir well. Add the pod too.

Leave the sugar to infuse for a week or two. There is no need to remove the vanilla pod. As you use the sugar, you can top it up with more, so that you have a constant supply.

• Sprinkle over strawberries

• Sweeten whipped cream

• Use a spoonful in baking in place of regular sugar

• Dust over mince pies at Christmas

• Try a spoonful in your coffee

• Flavour icing for cakes

• Make custard or crème brûlée

• Use it to sweeten cocoa

• Whip up some homemade vanilla ice cream

Cinnamon toast *(three ways)*

Buttery, sugary, warmly spiced toast – the kind that demands to be eaten on a winter afternoon in front of a crackling fire. Or indeed to be made over the fire, for it seems that cinnamon toast is a pleasure that has been around for several hundred years. Allow 1–2 slices of bread per person.

Historical

First published in 1660, Robert May's *The Accomplisht Cook or The Art and Mystery of Cookery* contains a recipe that involves making a paste of cinnamon, sugar and claret, spreading it onto thin toast and warming it over the fire. Here's an adaptation for the 21st century.

1 tbsp red wine

3 tbsp cinnamon sugar (page 140)

2–3 slices of bread (white or brown)

1 Preheat the oven to 190°C (375°F). Mix the wine and cinnamon sugar together in a small bowl to make a spreadable paste. Adjust the quantities if it is too thick or runny.

2 Lightly toast some bread (thinly sliced, if you want to be authentic). Spread the paste on the toast. Place the slices on a baking tray and warm in the oven for 5–10 minutes (5 minutes warms it; 10 will give you a slight crust). Eat hot (it's not bad cold either).

Eggy

'French Toast', 'Eggy Bread' – call it what you will, cinnamon loves it and this makes a great breakfast dish. The Tasting Panel claims that it tastes a bit like pancakes.

1 large egg

3 tbsp milk

4 tsp cinnamon sugar (page 140)

3 slices white bread, cut in half

25 g (1 oz) butter

1 Beat the egg, milk and 1 teaspoon of the cinnamon sugar in a shallow bowl. Lay the bread in the egg mixture, turning the slices over and making sure that each piece is thoroughly coated and the mixture has all been absorbed.

2 Melt the butter in a frying pan and fry the bread for 2–3 minutes on each side, until golden brown.

3 Sprinkle the remaining cinnamon sugar over the toast and eat hot.

Super-speedy

This is very good topped with thickly sliced bananas.

2–3 thick slices of white bread

25 g (1 oz) butter

4 tsp cinnamon sugar (page 140)

1 Take as many thick slices of good white bread as you want to eat and toast lightly.

2 Spread liberally with butter and sprinkle generously with cinnamon sugar.

3 If you can wait, put the cinnamon toast under a hot grill for a few minutes until lightly caramelized. (If not, eat straight away.)

Banana cake *with cinnamon sugar*

Over-ripe bananas mean only one thing in our house – cake! This one is best eaten fresh and warm from the oven. The sugary crust came about by a slip of the hand, and what was intended as a light sprinkling of cinnamon sugar became a thick layer. It met with great approval, so that's the way I always make it now.

150 g (5½ oz) butter or margarine

150 g (5½ oz) sugar

2 eggs

1 tsp vanilla extract

150 g (5½ oz) self-raising flour

2–3 very ripe bananas

2 tbsp cinnamon sugar (page 140)

You should get about 12–15 slices, but I have to warn you, this is the fastest-disappearing cake in our house.

1 Preheat the oven to 180°C (350°F). Line a 20 cm (8 in) square cake tin with baking parchment.

2 Beat the butter or margarine and sugar together. Beat in the eggs one at a time and stir in the vanilla.

3 Gently stir in the flour until thoroughly combined, then beat the mixture well.

4 Mash the bananas well with a fork, then stir them into the cake mixture. Tip it into the cake tin and sprinkle the top liberally with cinnamon sugar.

5 Bake for about 30 minutes. Lift the cake out of the tin and leave to cool on a wire rack.

VARIATIONS

This recipe also works very well with light brown flour.

For special occasions, spread a layer of thick caramel sauce such as Dulce de Leche on top and decorate with banana slices (dip these in lemon juice first so they do not discolour), then sprinkle cinnamon sugar on top.

Herb teas

Infusions of herbs have been used for centuries to cure all manner of ailments, though these days they are just as likely to be served in restaurants as an alternative to a post-dinner coffee. Once the stuff of health food shops, they are now stocked in every supermarket. Fresh or dried herbs can be used.

PICKING

Herbs are at their best if picked on a warm dry day, after the dew has evaporated but before they are in full sun.

DRYING

Spread the leaves on a clean cloth or brown paper on a wire rack so that air can circulate. Leave in a warm dry place until they have fully dried out. This can take a few days or longer, depending on the herb and the drying conditions. Alternatively, tie in small bunches and hang by their stems. Once dried, store in clean dry jars in a cool dark place.

BREWING

Use a separate teapot, if possible. If you make tea in a mug or cup, cover it so that the precious oils that evaporate in steam are not lost. For a pot you will need about 600 ml (1 pint) boiling water to 20 g (¾ oz) dried herbs, or to 30 g (1 oz) fresh herbs. For a cup you'll need 1–2 tsp dried or 2–3 tsp fresh herbs per cup. Pour boiling water over and leave to infuse for 10 minutes.

Camomile tea

Made from the flowers. Very soothing on the stomach, this is what we were always given for upset tummies. It is also a calming bedtime drink. For congestion caused by colds and flu, or a cough that keeps you awake at night, make a cup of camomile tea and stir in some honey, then sip slowly (as hot as possible) while inhaling the steam.

For tired eyes soak a cotton handkerchief or cotton wool in lukewarm tea and apply to the eyelids for 10 minutes (make sure there are no stray bits of camomile in the tea). Or use camomile tea bags.

Peppermint tea

Refreshing, stimulating and good for the digestion. Try it the Moroccan way, heavily sweetened and served in small tea glasses. A tea made from equal amounts of peppermint, yarrow and elderflower is a traditional cold and flu cure.

Sage tea

Sage has antiseptic properties and this makes it an excellent remedy for sore throats or a sore mouth. It is more commonly used for gargling than drinking. Gargle about 100 ml (3½ fl oz) two to three times a day, or sweeten with honey and sip.

CAUTION

Herbs can be potent. Do not over-indulge and if in any doubt, consult a health professional, especially if destined for children and the elderly. Herbs should not be used in pregnancy without seeking medical advice first.

Wild

Elderflowers, blackberries, dandelions and horseradish

Cordials

A glut of ripe berries, cooked just long enough to release their juice, will make a cordial that allows the natural flavours and colours of the fruit to shine through. Capture the delicate summer fragrance of elderflowers, their season all too brief, by steeping them in a lemony syrup for a day before bottling. Harder fruits, such as apples and pears, can be used too, though they are best in combination with something juicier, and you will need to use more water in the initial cooking to coax out the juice. Get creative and cook up your own combinations: pear and raspberry, summer berries, strawberry and rhubarb.

Cordials are not great keepers; they should be refrigerated and will be alright for one to two months that way. If you have made a small amount, this is not usually a problem, but larger quantities present more of a challenge. There are two ways to keep cordials long-term: freezing and pasteurization (pages 16–17). If you want elderflower cordial to see you through beyond the summer, you will need to opt for one of those methods.

Now, what to do with those lovely bottles of cordial? Drink them, diluted to taste with still or sparkling water – an excellent non-alcoholic alternative at parties and popular with children too. Mix with milk for a brilliant instant milkshake. In winter, dilute darker-hued cordials with boiling water for a warming drink. For something stronger, top them up with chilled champagne or sparkling wine. Add a splash to tiny glasses of ice-cold vodka. And if you have any left, use a little to sweeten a fruit salad, drizzle over ice creams and sorbets, stir a little into the fruit layer of a crumble. As the colours are intense a few drops can be used as a natural food colouring. Isn't that just the icing on the cake?

Elderflower cordial

The taste of early summer captured in a bottle. Pick the elderflowers on a warm sunny day, selecting fragrant creamy heads of flowers that are only just opening. Avoid any with brown blossoms, gather from trees that are well away from roads and pick only those at shoulder height and above.

1 Gently rinse the elderflowers to remove any little 'friends'.

2 Heat the sugar and water in a large saucepan, stirring until the sugar is dissolved. Bring briefly to the boil, then turn off the heat.

3 Place the elderflower heads and lemon slices in a large bowl and pour the sugar syrup over them. Stir in the citric acid, cover with a cloth and leave to infuse for 24–48 hours.

4 Strain the cordial through a scalded jelly bag (page 12) or a muslin-lined sieve, then pour it into sterilized bottles (page 18) and store in the fridge.

I usually make a large quantity and pasteurize the bottles (page 17) so that they will, in theory, last the year. Usually they are all gone before January.

VARIATION

Add a couple of slices of fresh root ginger to the mixture.

25 elderflower heads

1.7 kg (3 lb 12 oz) white granulated sugar

1.2 litres (2 pints) water

2 lemons (unwaxed, organic if possible), sliced

75 g (2½ oz) citric acid

Makes about 1.5 litres (2¾ pints)

Keeps for 2 months unopened in the fridge

Blackberry cordial

Juicy blackberries make a beautiful deep-coloured cordial. Dilute with hot water for a warming drink on a winter evening, maybe with a splash of whisky or rum. Drizzle neat over ice creams and sorbets, add to a bowl of berries, or use in white wine to make Kir.

1 kg (2 lb 4 oz) blackberries

juice of ½ lemon, plus a little more to taste

200 ml (7 fl oz) water

350–450 g (12 oz–1 lb) white granulated sugar

Makes about 800 ml (1½ pints)

Keeps for up to 5 weeks unopened in the fridge. Once opened, use within 2–3 weeks

1 Wash the blackberries briefly, then put them in a large pan with the lemon juice and the water. Bring slowly to the boil, then lower the heat and simmer gently for 10–15 minutes until the fruit is very soft. Mash the fruit a little while it is simmering.

2 Pour into a scalded jelly bag (page 12) or a sieve lined with muslin, and leave it to drip for 2 hours into a large bowl or jug. Press the fruit purée down in the bag to extract all the juice.

3 Measure the juice and pour it into the cleaned pan. You should have around 500–600 ml (18–20 fl oz). Weigh out the sugar: you need about 300–350 g (10½–12 oz) of sugar per 500 ml (18 fl oz) juice. Heat gently and stir until the sugar is completely dissolved. Scrape down the sides with a spatula now and then.

4 Taste, and add a squeeze more lemon juice if necessary. Using a funnel, fill hot sterilized bottles (page 18) to within 1 cm (½ in) of the top, leave to cool and then store in the fridge.

TIP

Cooking with blackberries can be a messy business. Wipe up any splashes as soon as possible for the juice will stain any porous surface.

VARIATION

Substitute a handful of elderberries for some of the blackberries.

Foraging

There is such pleasure to be had in gathering something delicious and naturally grown, and all for free too. Scratches and scrapes, an encounter with a stinging nettle or two, are all part of the fun; I see it as nature's way of exacting a small payment for the goods. The countryside is full of edibles, but there are foraging opportunities aplenty for city-dwellers too. Juicy blackberries, heavy heads of elderflower in spring and their berries in autumn and wild horseradish in abundance are all to be found within a 15-minute walk from our home in the London suburbs. Always gather from plants that are well away from roads and take only what you need.

Of course, you need to know what you're picking (and make sure you have permission from the landowner if necessary). Ben looks on in alarm as Alexander stuffs berries into his mouth, but I'm confident that our youngest knows what he is doing; he's hunted for blueberries ever since he could walk. Stick to the things you can identify with complete confidence, such as blackberries – one of our best-known and readily available wild foods. If you are lucky enough to find them by the kilo, there are plenty of recipes that call for large quantities of them. And if you only manage to get a small bag, a few berries can go a long way. Freeze them on a baking tray after picking (so that they are frozen individually, rather than in a big lump), then transfer to a lidded container. Just a few will add colour and flavour to an apple pie or crumble. Crush the juice from a couple of blackberries to colour icing or an apple jelly; decorate a pudding; cook a handful with meat.

Wild foods are not only acceptable once more, they have become downright fashionable, even featuring on the menus of top restaurants. With more adventurous eating habits, and perhaps nudged by a little economic hardship, increasing numbers of us are heading for the hedgerows, secateurs in hand.

Autumn chutney

This is a flexible recipe, ideal for using up different fruits at the beginning of autumn. A bit more of one fruit, a little less of the other will make no odds. The produce can be varied too – try marrow, red or green tomatoes, pears, greengages or damsons. It is a good all-rounder for serving with cold meats and cheeses, and I have been known to stir half a jar of it into a beef casserole.

300 g (10½ oz) onions, chopped

700 g (1 lb 9 oz) plums, stoned and quartered

600 g (1 lb 5 oz) cooking apples, peeled, cored and chopped

350 g (12 oz) blackberries

75 g (2½ oz) elderberries

600 ml (1 pint) red wine vinegar

125 g (4½ oz) raisins

350 g (12 oz) soft light brown sugar

1 tsp allspice

1 tsp cinnamon

1 tsp ginger

1 tsp coriander

a pinch of sea salt

a pinch of chilli flakes
(more, if you like it hot)

Makes about 6 x 340 g (12 oz) jars

Keeps for 12 months

1 Put all the ingredients into a preserving pan and bring slowly to the boil, stirring. Make sure that all the sugar has dissolved.

2 Lower the heat and simmer for 1½–2 hours until the chutney is well reduced, stirring frequently. A wooden spoon drawn across the surface should leave a trail when it is ready. Cooking time can vary, since it depends somewhat on the ingredients used – some have more water content than others.

3 Pot into hot sterilized jars (page 18) and leave to mature for a few weeks before eating.

A NOTE ON STIRRING

As chutney reduces, it has more of a tendency to stick. A quick stir now and then in the beginning is fine, but as time passes you will need to tend the pot with more vigilance and stir frequently. Nothing is more irritating than to spend all that time preparing and simmering, only for it all to burn in the last 10 minutes because you went to check your e-mail.

Bramble jelly

Here is a gorgeous deep-coloured jelly that sets well and makes a fantastic filling for a sponge cake. If you can get hold of windfall cooking apples (ask your friends) and pick some blackberries, then this delicious jelly is also virtually free. Cheapskate that I am, that makes it all the more delicious.

1 kg (2 lb 4 oz) blackberries

2 large cooking apples, roughly chopped (no need to peel or core)

1 lemon

500 ml (18 fl oz) water

white granulated sugar

Makes about 4 x 340 g (12 oz) jars

Keeps for 9–12 months

1 Wash the blackberries and put them in a large pan with the apples. Squeeze the lemon and add the juice, peel and water to the pan. Heat slowly and simmer for about 15 minutes until soft.

2 Pour into a scalded jelly bag (page 12) and leave it to drip for a few hours or overnight. As this jelly is so dark, squeezing the bag does not matter so much as with paler jellies, and you do get a lot more juice – so go ahead and squeeze if you like.

3 Measure the juice and pour it into the cleaned pan. Add sugar accordingly – 500 g (1 lb 2 oz) sugar for every 500 ml (18 fl oz) juice. Warm gently and stir until the sugar is dissolved, then turn up the heat and bring to a fast boil. Cook for 3–5 minutes, then test for a set and pot into hot sterilized jars (page 18).

VARIATIONS

Bramble jelly with sloe gin

Stir 2 tbsp sloe gin into the jelly once setting point has been reached.

Hedgerow jelly

Use a combination of blackberries and elderberries in roughly equal quantities. This makes a deliciously dark, flavoursome jelly.

Potato and dandelion salad

Rich in vitamins and minerals, dandelions are known for their diuretic and cleansing properties. My mother would often pick dandelion leaves to add a little fresh green tang to a potato salad. I gather a handful from the garden for the first salad of the year in February, long before any cultivated salad leaves are thought of. Pick young leaves; older ones can be bitter.

1 kg (2 lb 4 oz) waxy potatoes

1 small onion, finely chopped

3 small gherkins

1 eating apple
(a crunchy red one for preference)

a small handful young
dandelion leaves

For the dressing

3 tbsp cider vinegar

2 tbsp mild olive oil

a pinch of salt

1 tsp white sugar

100 ml (3½ fl oz) boiling water

Serves 6–8

1 Boil potatoes in their skins until just cooked (about 15–20 minutes). Leave them to cool for 20 minutes, then pull the skins off the warm potatoes with a knife, slicing them into a serving bowl as you go.

2 Whisk together the dressing ingredients and taste – adjust with a little more salt, sugar or a touch of mustard if necessary. Pour the dressing over the warm potatoes, stir gently, then cover and leave to soak up the dressing for 30 minutes.

3 Meanwhile, chop the onion, cut up the gherkins into rounds or dice and cut the apples into small slices. Wash the dandelion leaves and pat dry, then cut or tear them into small pieces.

4 Gently stir the onion, gherkin, apple and dandelion leaves into the salad. Serve warm or at room temperature. Any leftovers are not bad the next day either.

Czech ham rolls *with horseradish*
(Šunkové Rolky)

Even the smallest greengrocer's shop in Prague sells fresh horseradish roots and this pungent tuber is almost certain to appear on the menu in any Czech restaurant. Ham rolls filled with a tasty horseradish cream are a traditional Czech starter and a popular choice at weddings. It is rare to see horseradish roots on sale in England, but luckily for me it grows wild on our allotments.

100 g (3½ oz) cream cheese or curd cheese

150 ml (5 fl oz) double or whipping cream

1–2 tbsp fresh horseradish root

8 small slices of good-quality ham

tomatoes, salad leaves, parsley, to garnish

Serves 4 as a starter or 2 as a supper with salad and bread and butter

1 Peel the horseradish root with a potato peeler. Minimize the fumes by keeping it submerged in water while you peel. Grate finely, holding it at arm's length.

2 Beat the cream cheese until softened, then stir in the grated horseradish. The amount of horseradish required depends a lot on its strength and your taste, so start with a little and adjust accordingly.

3 Whip the cream and fold into the cream cheese/horseradish mix.

4 Place a spoonful of the horseradish cream on each slice of ham and roll up. Garnish with salad.

TIPS

Horseradish is strong stuff and will make your eyes water. Wear gloves and open the windows when preparing.

If you cannot get fresh horseradish, use 1–2 tbsp horseradish sauce. Again, as these vary in strength, adjust according to taste.

To make a larger amount to keep, mix the grated horseradish with a little white wine vinegar (about 1 tbsp vinegar to 3 tbsp horseradish), add a pinch of salt and sugar, and keep in a sterilized jar in the fridge for up to six months.

Peter Rabbit's summer pudding

This is a slapdash version of the traditional Summer Pudding. After reading *The Tale of Peter Rabbit* to the children one day, they were taken by the idea of having bread and milk and blackberries for tea so I came up with this recipe. Thick pouring cream would be my ideal accompaniment, but really creamy milk is also good. Poor Peter – he didn't get to eat it of course. He was tucked up in bed with a dose of camomile tea…

800 g (1 lb 12 oz) blackberries

125 g (4½ oz) golden caster sugar

a pinch of cinnamon or mixed spice

3 tbsp water

7 slices from a day-old loaf of white bread, cut 1 cm (½ in) thick, crusts removed

2 tbsp blackberry liqueur, blackberry cordial or other good-quality fruit cordial (or reserve 2 tbsp juice from the cooked blackberries)

thick pouring cream, to serve

Serves 6–8

1 Place the blackberries, sugar and spice in a saucepan with 3 tbsp of water and simmer gently for about 3 minutes. Leave to cool for an hour or so.

2 Line the bottom of a dish with bread (cut and tear it to fit), and spoon some of the blackberries and juice over it. Continue to layer bread and blackberries in the dish, ending with a layer of bread. Spoon the cordial, liqueur or juice over the top, and press down well so that the top layer is thoroughly soaked. If you have time, place a weight on top and leave the pudding for a few hours or overnight before serving. But if you cannot wait, just enjoy as it is.

3 Serve bowls of blackberry pudding to your bunnies with plenty of cream.

VARIATION

You can use this method to make a cheat's Summer Pudding too. Just use a mixture of summer berries (strawberries, raspberries, redcurrants, blackcurrants) instead of blackberries.

Intoxicating

Alcoholic drinks

Liqueurs and other strong stuff

Homemade liqueurs are fun to make, ideal to give as presents and utterly delicious.
Several of my favourites are included in this book, and if you enjoy making these
there are many more out there waiting to be tried – crème de cassis, raspberry gin
and limoncello, to name but a few.

Flavoured vodkas have become very fashionable and making them is simplicity
itself. This pure, clear spirit is an excellent base in which to capture the essence of
added ingredients and almost anything can be used as a flavouring: fruit of all kinds,
herbs, spices, horseradish, chillies, rose petals, honey, even chocolate. I find it best to
use only one or two additions per bottle. The high alcohol content of the vodka acts
as a preservative, so if you choose to leave your additions in the bottles rather than
straining them out, they will keep perfectly. A tiny glass of freezer-cold cranberry
vodka, with a tartly alcoholic cranberry or two in the glass, makes a fantastic
Christmas aperitif.

The recipe for cream liqueur is something of a 1970s throwback; it's great
though, and will give any of the famous brands a run for their money. Serve over ice
or mix with cherry juice for a long drink; add a shot to coffee; pour it over ice
cream… Come to think of it, make it *into* ice cream.

Our mother had a superb command of the English language, but certain things
were known only by their German names; Glühwein is one of them. I don't
remember hearing the term 'mulled wine' until late into my teens, though Glühwein
was a concept from an early age. It's not something to make and keep, but to make
and drink hot on any cold day. It will warm you from the very tips of your toes. The
blackberry liqueur also seems to be more of a winter's drink, and would do well as a
toddy, topped up with hot water and a little extra brandy. Whichever takes your
fancy, this is strong stuff; a little goes a long way. Sip slowly and enjoy.

Flavoured vodkas

To make these, I usually buy a large bottle of vodka and decant it into smaller bottles, each of a different flavour. There is no need to get the most expensive spirit – a good quality own-brand is fine. As for the flavourings, let your imagination take over.

General method

1 Put the ingredients in the bottle first, then top up with vodka. Close tightly and shake. Leave to infuse somewhere dark and dry for at least a week (a month is better). Shake occasionally.

2 For fruit vodkas, use 225–350 g (8–12 oz) fruit and 3 tbsp white granulated or caster sugar to each 750 ml (26 fl oz) vodka.

3 Once the vodkas have reached their required strength, you can strain them or leave the extras in the bottles. Be warned that the flavours will continue to strengthen – which makes quite a difference with potent ingredients, such as chillies.

4 Store in the freezer (they will not freeze solid, but will be ice-cold) and serve in small gorgeous glasses.

All the recipes here are for a 250 ml (9 fl oz) bottle

Raspberry vodka

Soft fruits make delicious and beautiful vodkas. Try making this with others, such as blackberries and redcurrants.

60 g (2¼ oz) raspberries

30 g (1 oz) sugar

Put the sugar and fruit in the bottle and top up with vodka. Shake gently so that the berries don't disintegrate.

Cranberry vodka

A lovely Christmas aperitif, served ice cold in small glasses.

50 g (1¾ oz) cranberries

40 g (1½ oz) sugar

Use it to make a Sea Breeze cocktail: 2 parts cranberry vodka, 3 parts cranberry juice, 3 parts grapefruit juice. Serve over ice and garnish with lime.

Chilli vodka

A vodka with a kick – the perfect base for the Best Bloody Mary (page 168).

1 large chilli

Prick the chilli with a fork or skewer and push it into the bottle. Fill the bottle with vodka. This vodka will get stronger over time, so you may want to remove the chilli once it is spicy enough for you.

Vanilla spice vodka

I tried a vanilla vodka at a Polish restaurant in London, which had over 40 varieties on offer. It was hard to choose…

20 g (¾ oz) cinnamon sugar

1 used vanilla pod or ½ a new one

Put the sugar and vanilla pod in the bottle and top up with vodka.

Citrus vodka

A favourite of mine. Pare the fruit with a potato peeler – try to get long, wide strips. Experiment with other citrus fruits too, such as mandarin and grapefruit.

2 strips of lemon peel

2 strips of lime peel

30 g (1 oz) sugar

Put the peel into the bottle, add the sugar then top up with vodka.

Spiced blackberry liqueur

Several years ago we received a bottle of wonderful, sweet and spicy homemade liqueur at Christmas from my husband's niece, who has kindly shared her recipe with me. This recipe makes enough for a large bottle for yourself and a few smaller ones to give away.

1.75 kg (3 lb 13 oz) blackberries

550 ml (19 fl oz) water

1 tbsp whole cloves

1 tbsp grated nutmeg

2 large cinnamon sticks

900 g (2 lb) white granulated sugar

300–350 ml (10–12 fl oz) brandy

**Makes about 2 litres
(3½ pints)**

Keeps for 12 months

1 Place the blackberries, water and spices in a large pan. Cover and bring to the boil, then reduce the heat and simmer for 15 minutes until the blackberries are soft.

2 Strain through a scalded jelly bag or a sieve lined with muslin. Leave to drip for about 1 hour.

3 Measure the juice and pour it into the cleaned pan. Add 500 g (1 lb 2 oz) of sugar for every 600 ml (1 pint) juice. Heat gently and stir well to dissolve the sugar.

4 Stir in 300 ml (10 fl oz) of the brandy. Taste, and add a little more brandy if required. Strain again through the clean jelly bag or sieve before bottling up (page 18).

Best Bloody Mary

The extras in a Bloody Mary are a matter of personal taste; this is a recipe to suggest, rather than to dictate. Sherry can create very different results depending on the variety used – Amontillado or Fino work very well here, but experiment. Depending on the strength of your chilli vodka, you may like a few drops of Tabasco sauce too. A fine grinding of pepper also tastes good.

3–4 ice cubes

50 ml (2 fl oz) chilli vodka

40 ml (1½ fl oz) sherry
(Fino or Amontillado)

200 ml (7 fl oz) chilled tomato juice

a good squeeze of lime juice and a
lime wedge to serve

a shake of Worcestershire sauce,
to taste

a few drops Tabasco sauce
(optional)

Makes 1 glass

1 Put the ice in a tall glass. Pour over the vodka and sherry, and top up with tomato juice. Add the lime juice, lime wedge and Worcestershire sauce, and stir. Taste and add Tabasco if required.

Great to make in a large jug for a crowd – leave bottles of Worcestershire sauce, Tabasco and lime wedges to hand, so that each person can season to taste.

VARIATION

This makes a pretty potent cocktail. You can decrease the booze and increase the juice for something a little less intoxicating.

Edward: 'What's a Bloody Mary?'

James: 'It's Mummy when she gets cross.'

Jarka's cream liqueur

This is usually prepared with Czech *tuzemák*, a rum-like spirit distilled from potatoes or sugar beet. Boiling up cans of condensed milk seems rather out of keeping with the nature of this book, but I couldn't resist. The quantities can easily be doubled if you want to make a large batch.

500 ml (18 fl oz) dark rum, whisky or brandy

1 tin sweetened condensed milk, approx 400 ml (14 fl oz)

1 tin evaporated milk, approx 400 ml (14 fl oz)

Makes 1.3 litres (2¼ pints)

Keeps for up to 12 months, though it may thicken a little over time. Store somewhere cool and dark.

1 Place the tin of sweetened condensed milk in a saucepan and cover with water. Bring to the boil and simmer for 2 hours, turning the tin over occasionally and topping up with more water if necessary – the tin must always be submerged. Then remove from the pan (using tongs or a cloth) and allow to cool.

2 Open the tin and scoop the contents (which will have thickened to a caramel) into a large bowl. Add the evaporated milk, then whisk to a smooth consistency using a hand-held mixer. The mixture does splatter rather, so use a large bowl and start whisking on a low setting.

3 Add the spirit and whisk well until combined. Pour the liqueur into sterilized bottles and allow to stand for a few days. Serve chilled.

Glühwein

Advent marks the beginning of the Glühwein season in Germany and its equivalent in many other European countries: outdoor Christmas markets set up their stalls, and hot spiced wine is the perfect drink to warm you up while browsing. My mother sometimes called it 'Glow Wine', which I think is rather appropriate.

750 ml (26 fl oz) bottle red wine

250 ml (9 fl oz) water

2 cinnamon sticks

10 cloves

½ a star anise

a few strips of lemon peel

2–3 tbsp white granulated sugar

Enough for 5–6 servings

1 Put the wine and water into a saucepan. Add the spices – I leave them to drift, as I do not mind a stray clove in my drink, but you can tie them in muslin if you prefer.

2 Heat gently. When the wine is hot, add sugar to taste, and stir until dissolved. Continue to heat until the wine is almost at boiling point (but do not allow it to boil, or the alcohol will evaporate). Serve it very hot, in ceramic cups or heat-proof glasses.

VARIATION

Vary the spices – try mace, nutmeg and cardamom. Add slices of orange and lemon.

Daily bread

Loaves, rolls, scones and muffins

Bread

'If thou tastest a crust of bread, thou tastest
all the stars and all the heavens.'

Robert Browning (1812–1889)

Home-baked bread is a particular domestic delight; the smell of baking bread creates
a sense of warmth and wellbeing not easily matched. A crusty loaf, newly emerged
from the oven, with some good butter and a fine preserve, is a simple feast to rival
the grandest meal. While bread-making machines have enabled more people to enjoy
their own homemade bread, they reinforce the notion that making it the traditional
way (in a bowl, with your hands) is difficult and hard work. It really isn't; and
although the process is lengthy your effort is only required for a fraction of the
overall time.

Turning out uniform loaves one at a time is not what I want. For me, the joy
of making my own bread comes from the connection with the dough, the mixing,
kneading, punching and the slight unpredictability of the final outcome. A little
wonkiness is good. And I love the fact that I can make several loaves at once. Bread
freezes well and defrosts quickly, so a morning's effort means a supply of homemade
loaves to enjoy over the coming days.

A basic loaf needs only a few ingredients: strong bread flour, yeast, salt, oil or
margarine, water (one part boiling to two parts cold), a little effort to knead the
dough until smooth and elastic (ten minutes should do it), a warm place to rise and
a nice hot oven. And time. Although the whole process can take 2½–3 hours from
start to finish, your involvement amounts to around 30 minutes of that. In between
mixing, kneading and knocking back, you can have cups of tea and put your feet up,
until it is time to take the crusty (and, I hope, a little wonky) loaves out of the oven
and admire your handiwork.

Basic white bread

This is my fail-safe recipe for white bread. It makes three big loaves, one to eat right now and two to freeze. The Tasting Panel has been known to demolish an entire loaf in one sitting.

1.5 kg (3 lb 5 oz) strong white bread flour, plus a little extra for kneading

3 tsp salt

2 x 7 g (¼ oz) sachets dried yeast

2 tsp sugar

1 tbsp olive or sunflower oil or 30 g (1 oz) margarine

900 ml (30 fl oz) warm water

a little extra oil

Makes 3 large or 4 small loaves

1 In a large mixing bowl, stir the flour, salt, yeast and sugar together. Mix in the oil or rub in the margarine with your fingers.

2 Make a well in the flour mix and pour in the water. Stir it in, until most of the flour has been absorbed. Then ditch the spoon and work the dough with your hands, bringing it all together and beginning to knead it in the bowl.

3 Flour a work surface and tip the dough out of the bowl. Now for serious kneading: push the dough with the heels of your hands and fold in half towards you. Do this 2 to 3 times, then give it a quarter turn, push and fold again. You will soon get into the rhythm. Keep going until the dough is smooth and elastic (about 5–10 minutes).

4 Put the dough back in the bowl, rub a thin layer of oil over it, and cover with a clean cloth or cling film. Leave it to rise for about 1–1½ hours until it has doubled in size. Grease and flour three 900 g (2 lb), or four 450 g (1 lb) loaf tins or 2–3 baking sheets.

5 Now it's time for 'knocking back': tip the dough on to a floured surface and punch it vigorously until you have knocked the air out. Knead again for 2 minutes, then divide into 3 equal pieces. Form each piece into a loaf shape and place in a loaf tin or on a baking sheet. Make slashes in the top if you like. For a glossy finish, brush the tops with beaten egg or a little milk. Sprinkle with poppy or sesame seeds or leave plain. Preheat the oven to 230°C (450°F). Leave to rise for 30–40 minutes.

6 Bake for about 30 minutes. Smaller loaves will bake more quickly so check after 20 minutes. To check if the loaves are done, tap them on the bottom – they should make a hollow sound. Leave to cool on a wire rack.

Basic wholemeal bread

Wholemeal flour is much coarser than white, and the kneading takes a little more effort, but the method for making wholemeal bread is basically the same. For a lighter loaf, substitute a little strong white flour for some of the wholemeal. I like to top this bread with fine oats or oat bran.

1.5 kg (3 lb 5 oz) strong wholemeal bread flour, plus a little extra for kneading

3 tsp salt

2 x 7 g (¼ oz) sachets dried yeast

2 tsp sugar

1 tbsp olive oil or 30 g (1 oz) margarine

900 ml (30 fl oz) warm water

oats or oat bran, to sprinkle on top

Makes 3 large loaves

1–5 Follow the steps for basic white bread (opposite). Grease and flour three 900 g (2 lb) loaf tins or two baking sheets. Brush with water and scatter a little oatbran or fine oats on top, or just leave them as they are. Beaten egg or milk will give a shiny glaze.

6 Bake for 30–35 minutes. Leave to cool on a wire rack.

Pumpkin seed and carrot bread

I once bought a divine seedy carrot bread in Austria; dark, chewy and packed full of seeds. I experimented with my own version and, although it is nothing like the one I originally tasted, it's excellent. The addition of carrot makes this a moist loaf that keeps well. I usually make these 'free-form', patting the dough into round or oval loaves and baking them on a tray. They may take a little longer to bake if made in a loaf tin.

1 kg (2 lb 4 oz) brown bread flour, plus a little extra for kneading

2 tsp salt

2 x 7 g (¼ oz) sachet dried yeast

1 tsp sugar

4 tbsp mixed seeds (pumpkin, sunflower, linseed, sesame, hemp), plus 1–2 tbsp extra for sprinkling

2 large carrots, peeled and finely grated

1 tbsp olive oil

600 ml (1 pint) warm water

Makes 2 loaves

1 Stir together the flour, salt, yeast, sugar and seeds in a large mixing bowl. Rub in the grated carrot and olive oil, in much the same way as if you were making a crumble. Make sure the carrot is evenly distributed.

2 Pour in the water and stir well to incorporate the dry ingredients. Start to knead the dough with your hands in the bowl, then tip it out onto a floured surface and continue to knead for about 10 minutes until you have a smooth and elastic dough.

3 Oil the dough and leave it to rise (in a bowl covered with a tea towel or in a polythene bag) for about an hour until it has doubled in size.

4 Grease and flour a large baking sheet. Tip the dough onto a floured surface and punch to knock out the air. Knead it for 2–3 minutes, then divide the dough into 2 equal pieces. Form each piece into a loaf shape and place on the baking sheet. Brush with water and sprinkle the remaining seeds on top, pressing them down lightly. Preheat the oven to 230°C (450°F). Leave the loaves to rise for 30–40 minutes.

5 Bake for 25–30 minutes. To check if the loaves are done, tap them on the bottom – they should make a hollow sound. Leave to cool on a wire rack.

Poppy seed rolls

Rolls straight from the oven with plenty of butter (and jam, of course) are a real treat for breakfast. Unless you get up very early and breakfast late, it's a tall order to make these on the day, but you can easily reheat them – just place on a baking tray in a preheated oven at 200°C (400°F) for a few minutes.

1 kg (2 lb 4 oz) strong white bread flour, plus a little extra for kneading

2 tsp salt

1 x 7 g (¼ oz) sachet dried yeast

1 tsp sugar

35 g (1¼ oz) margarine or oil

300 ml (10 fl oz) hot water mixed with 300 ml (10 fl oz) cold milk

a little olive or vegetable oil

milk or beaten egg to glaze

4–5 tsp poppy seeds

Makes 16 medium-large rolls

1 In a large mixing bowl, stir together the flour, salt, yeast and sugar. Rub in the margarine.

2 Pour in the water and milk mixture and stir well. Knead the dough, in the bowl to begin with, then tip out onto a floured surface and continue kneading until smooth and stretchy (for about 5–10 minutes).

3 Oil the dough and leave it to rise, in a bowl covered with a tea towel or in a polythene bag, for about an hour until it has doubled in size.

4 Grease and flour 3 baking sheets. Tip the dough onto a floured surface and punch to knock out the air. Knead it for a couple of minutes and then divide into 16 equal pieces. Form each piece into the shape of your choice (mini loaves, knots, twists) and place, spaced well apart, on the baking sheets. Brush with beaten egg or milk and sprinkle generously with poppy seeds. Preheat the oven to 220°C (425°F). Leave the rolls to rise for 30–40 minutes.

5 Bake for 10–15 minutes. When done, they will sound hollow if tapped on the bottom. Leave to cool on a wire rack.

Focaccia

The addition of olive oil, both in and on the dough, makes this flat Italian bread deliciously moist and flavoursome. Strong-tasting woody herbs are my preference in this recipe, though basil is good too. It goes well with bowls of soup or pasta; or serve it as a starter, with a dish of olive oil as a dip.

500 g (1 lb 2 oz) strong white bread flour, plus a little extra for kneading

7 g (¼ oz) sachet dried yeast

1 tsp salt

225 ml (8 fl oz) warm water

75–100 ml (2½–3½ fl oz) olive oil

2 tsp dried herbs or 3–4 tsp chopped fresh herbs (eg rosemary, thyme, oregano or mixed herbs)

1 tsp coarse sea salt

freshly ground black pepper

Makes 2 focaccia

1 Mix the flour, yeast and salt in a large bowl. Stir in 50 ml (2 fl oz) of the olive oil and the water, and mix well to form a soft dough. Turn out onto a floured surface and knead until smooth (about 5 minutes).

2 Put the dough back in the bowl, rub a thin coating of oil over it, and cover with a clean tea towel or cling film. Leave it to rise for about an hour until it has doubled in size.

3 Grease a large baking sheet. Punch the dough down on a floured surface and knead briefly, then divide into two equal pieces. Roll or press each piece into a flat, oval shape and place them both onto the baking sheet.

4 Make indentations in the loaves, using a wooden spoon handle or a finger. Scatter the herbs over the breads, drizzle over the remaining oil, then sprinkle with sea salt and a grinding of black pepper. Preheat the oven to 220°C (430°F). Leave to rise again for 20–30 minutes.

5 Bake for about 15 minutes until golden, then cool on a wire rack.

VARIATION

Tomato and olive focaccia

At Step 4, press 12–14 halved cherry tomatoes (cut side up) into the indentations and scatter with a handful of sliced, pitted black olives. Sprinkle with mixed herbs, salt and pepper and a drizzle of olive oil.

Fruit and spice loaf

A fruity teatime bread with a hint of cinnamon spice. The dried fruit –
I favour apricots and vine fruits – gives it a chewy sweetness. Cut thick
slices and spread generously with butter and jam or honey. If you can serve
the loaf warm, so much the better; or toast it very lightly. Your house will
smell delicious while it is baking.

500 g (1 lb 2 oz) strong white bread
flour plus a little extra for kneading

1 x 7 g (¼ oz) sachet dried yeast

2 tbsp white granulated sugar

1 tsp salt

2 tsp mixed spice

1 tsp cinnamon

30 g (1 oz) margarine or butter

150 g (5½ oz) mixed dried fruit
(raisins, sultanas, currants, apricots,
dates)

150 ml (5 fl oz) warm water mixed
with 150 ml (5 fl oz) milk

1 tbsp runny honey

Makes 1 large loaf

1 Mix together the flour, yeast,
sugar, salt and spices. Rub in the
margarine, then stir in the
dried fruit.

2 Add the tepid liquid and mix to
a dough. Turn out onto a floured
surface and knead well until smooth
(about 10 minutes).

3 Oil the dough and leave it in a
bowl covered with a tea towel or in
a polythene bag to rise for about
an hour until it has doubled in size.

4 Tip the dough onto a floured
surface and punch the air out of it,
then knead for a couple of minutes.

5 Grease and flour a 900 g (2 lb)
loaf tin. Shape the dough into a loaf
and place in the prepared loaf tin.
Preheat the oven to 210°C (410°F).
Leave it to rise for another
30–40 minutes.

6 Bake for 30–35 minutes. Leave
it to cool a little on a wire rack,
then brush with honey while the
loaf is still warm. This can be rather
messy so stand the rack on a plate
to catch any drips.

Peanut loaf

Luckily for my university flatmate Stephen and me, our mothers shared a considerable talent for the art of the Food Parcel. Mine would contain homemade chocolate brownies, iced cherry buns, a pot of honey; Stephen's invariably contained a Peanut loaf. Thank you to Dorothy Jones for this recipe (and for all those food parcels I had the joy of sharing over the years).

1 egg

150 ml (5 fl oz) milk

2 rounded tsp yeast extract

90 g (3¼ oz) soft margarine or butter

240 g (8½ oz) self-raising flour

60 g (2¼ oz) salted peanuts, very roughly chopped

60 g (2¼ oz) pickled onions, roughly chopped

100 g (3½ oz) Cheddar cheese, grated, plus 20 g (¾ oz) for sprinkling

¼ tsp dried mixed herbs

Makes 1 loaf (about 12 slices)

1 Preheat oven to 180°C (350°F). Grease and line a 450 g (1 lb) loaf tin with baking parchment.

2 Whisk the egg, milk and yeast extract together in a mixing bowl.

3 Beat in the remaining ingredients until you have a sticky, cake-like dough. Tip into the loaf tin and smooth the top. Sprinkle on the remaining grated Cheddar.

4 Bake for approximately an hour until risen and firm.

Eat in one go, with plenty of butter. Or pack into a parcel and send to someone who needs cheering up.

Muffins *with jam, curd or marmalade*

These light-textured muffins can be whipped up in half an hour, and make a delicious treat for a weekend breakfast. It's an ideal recipe for using up all those half-eaten jars of preserves that over-crowd my fridge. Serve warm from the oven as they are, or cut them in half and spread with butter.

250 g (9 oz) self-raising flour

1 tsp baking powder

100 g (3½ oz) white granulated sugar

a pinch of salt

1 egg

200 ml (7 fl oz) milk

100 ml (3½ fl oz) vegetable oil

3 tbsp of jam, fruit curd or marmalade of your choice (all the same or different varieties)

Makes 12 muffins

1 Preheat the oven to 200°C (400°F) and grease a 12-hole muffin tin or line with muffin cases.

2 Stir the flour, baking powder, sugar and salt together in a mixing bowl.

3 In a separate bowl, beat the egg. Stir in the milk and oil, then pour into the dry ingredients and stir lightly until just moistened – for no more than 30 seconds. Do not over-mix or the muffins will not rise well. The mixture will be lumpy, but don't worry.

4 Spoon half the mixture into the 12 muffin cases, and place a dollop of jam, curd or marmalade in each. Divide the remaining mixture between the muffins, spooning it over the jam.

5 Bake for 15–20 minutes until risen and golden, then leave to cool on a wire rack.

Scones

Scones can be made with store cupboard ingredients in less than half an hour, no yeast or eggs required. You can eat them straight from the oven. And of course they are an essential part of the cream tea (page 38). Scones are great for children's baking sessions – all the fun of mixing, rubbing in and stamping out shapes, but quick enough to please impatient young cooks.

350 g (12 oz) self-raising flour

1 tsp baking powder

1 tbsp white granulated sugar

a pinch of salt

85 g (3 oz) margarine or butter

175 ml (6 fl oz) milk

1 egg, beaten (or a little extra milk) to glaze

Makes 11–12 scones

1 Preheat the oven to 220°C (425°F) and lightly grease and flour a baking tray.

2 Stir the flour, baking powder, sugar and salt together in a mixing bowl. Rub in the margarine or butter until the mixture resembles fine breadcrumbs.

3 Pour in the milk and combine to make a soft dough. A knife is a good tool to start with, but carry on with your hands. Work quickly and do not over-handle the dough.

4 Turn the dough out onto a floured surface and knead briefly. Pat it into a round, about 2 cm (¾ in) high. Stamp out circles with a straight-sided 5 cm (2 in) cutter, gather the scraps and keep going until you have used up all the dough. Place on the baking tray and brush the tops with milk or beaten egg.

5 Bake for about 10–12 minutes, until risen and golden. These are best eaten warm or on the day of baking. If there are any left, they can be frozen.

TIP

Milk that is just starting to turn sour works perfectly in scone recipes.

VARIATIONS

For cheese scones, omit the sugar and stir in 100 g (3½ oz) grated Cheddar cheese at the end of step 2. Lightly press a little extra grated Cheddar onto each scone before baking.

For fruit scones, add 75 g (2½ oz) sultanas or chopped dates at the end of Step 2.

Cheesy scone bread

My mother made a deliciously dense, scone-like bread. Recently our friend David reintroduced us to the delights of this loaf, which the Tasting Panel adore. They will wait surprisingly patiently at the table for it to appear. Best served straight from the oven with lots of butter and more cheese.

500 g (1 lb 2 oz) self-raising flour

a pinch of salt

125 g (4½ oz) margarine or butter

125 g (4½ oz) Cheddar cheese, grated, plus a little more to sprinkle on top

300 ml (10 fl oz) milk

Serves 3 hungry boys and their parents (or 6–8 more restrained people)

1 Preheat the oven to 200°C (400°F). Grease and flour a baking tray or line with baking paper.

2 Put the flour and salt in a large mixing bowl and rub in the margarine or butter so that it resembles very fine breadcrumbs. Stir in the grated Cheddar.

3 Stir in the milk and combine to make a smooth dough. It is easiest to do this with your hands. Keep the flour handy as you may need to work in a little more if the dough is sticky.

4 Turn out onto a floured surface and knead briefly. Pat it into a round, no more than 2 cm (¾ in) high and put it on the baking tray. Brush with a little milk and sprinkle on the remaining Cheddar.

5 Bake for 30–45 minutes and eat warm, if possible.

TIP

If you are in a real hurry, divide the dough into several pieces before baking – they will take about 20 minutes to cook.

VARIATIONS

I nearly always make this with cheese, but you can leave it out for a plain scone bread.

Try adding a big spoonful of poppy seeds or a handful of chopped chives (or other herbs).

For a sweet version, omit the cheese and add a dessertspoonful of sugar and 125 g (4½ oz) sultanas or chopped dates.

Index

Acknowledgements

Huge thanks to:

My editor Sam Stanley for encouraging me to spend even more time than usual in two of my favourite pursuits – stirring the preserving pan and tapping at the keyboard; Geoff Borin for his gorgeous designs; John Davis for the beautiful photography; and Clare Sayer at New Holland for bringing the delights of preserving to a wider audience.

My friends, relatives, neighbours and plot-holders at Cole Park Allotments for the fruit and vegetables which appear on my doorstep, and for the recipes which they share with me. Keep up the good work.

My brother John, for his enthusiastic support throughout.

The Tasting Panel (Ben, Edward, James and Alexander) for eating it all, and for their honesty.

Notes from the Jam Cupboard could not have been written had I not had the good fortune to be brought up by an extraordinary person. I dedicate this book to the memory of my mother.

Renate Lindenthal Tregellas
1926–2006